# 21 KITCHENS
## A MEMOIR WITH RECIPES

This is the story of cooking in nine different states and twenty-one different kitchens. It is about food, location, politics, family and life.

By Lynn Halperin

Illustrations: Joe Halperin
Cover design: Jonathan Halperin

# CONTENTS

| | | |
|---|---|---|
| RECIPE INDEX | PAGE 242 | |
| | | KITCHEN COUNT |
| BOSTON | PAGE 8 | 2 |
| ROXBURY | PAGE 17 | 3 |
| MINNEAPOLIS (ST. LOUIS PARK) | PAGE 32 | 4 |
| MINNEAPOLIS (DINKYTOWN) | PAGE 35 | 5 |
| MINNEAPOLIS (NORTHEAST) | PAGE 44 | 6 |
| LEAVENWORTH | PAGE 51 | 7 |
| MARBLEHEAD (3 KITCHENS) | PAGE 81 | 10 |
| SUGARLOAF | PAGE 104 | 11 |
| RANGELEY | PAGE 106 | 12 |
| GREENSBORO & FLOYD | PAGE 131 | 14 |
| KIRKLAND | PAGE 158 | 15 |
| NEVADA CITY | PAGE 161 | 16 |
| PENN VALLEY | PAGE 163 | 17 |
| BERKELEY | PAGE 170 | 18 |
| OAKLAND | PAGE 176 | 19 |
| BALTIMORE | PAGE 200 | 20 AND 21 |

# TWENTY-ONE KITCHENS
## PROLOGUE

A memoir of kitchens and food: a story that starts when I was 20 in my first kitchen and ends while I am 72 in kitchen number 21, knowing there may be more to come. There were, of course, kitchens before this story begins. There were my mother's kitchens, kitchens that bring different kinds of memories and paint a different picture. The following is a small peek into that backstory before the adventure of my 21 Kitchens.

My mother, Esther, was the sixth of seven children of Russian Jewish immigrants. She was born in Troy, New York, but spent her late teen and early adult years in Washington, DC. Her father was a jeweler and her mother stayed at home trying to run a house on little money. It was a family rich in culture—violinists, opera singers and painters. My mother was an athlete and dancer. It was also a family that held some strong beliefs that were not always in the mainstream. Many were vegetarian generations before it became popular. My mother's eldest brother, who also converted the family to being secular and socialists, studied with Dr. Kellogg in Battle Creek, Michigan. By the time my mother was 11, there was no meat, chicken or fish, and everyone believed they had found the answer to immortality. I remember my grandparents as elderly and in failing health but I had the sense that, even when younger, they were no longer the leaders of their family having relinquished much control to their first-born son.

Her elder brother and his beliefs awed my mother, being young and impressionable. She chose to make all he said the cornerstone of her beliefs for the rest of her life. I remember her calling him whenever there were problems in our home. She would close the bedroom door and ask him what she should do about the "crisis" of the moment. I hated that and never respected his answers. I am sure much of my feelings toward him were strongly influenced by my dad who made no secret about his resentment of this relationship. Every time there was a visit with my uncle and his family my parents fought, before they came and after they left. I did love my aunt and four cousins so I always had mixed feelings. My mother lived to 93 years old and it was only the last six months of her life that she would ask, in moments when she felt vulnerable, if she had done something wrong. She wondered if she had misunderstood the rules to good health. She never thought she would be ill. Even though all but one sibling had died long before her, she still believed in the power of diet and atheism.

My mother had other passions that were more endearing to me. She was a great athlete, mostly tennis, and had a vast knowledge and interest in music and dance. She worked hard to bring culture to the community and was, I think, respected. She could also be fun. Most of the time she was loving to me because I was well behaved and, to the best of her knowledge, followed all her rules and beliefs. It wasn't until she saw me breaking away did I ever feel her control as a negative force. Those moments were painful.

My father, Charles, was also the sixth of seven children whose parents were also Jewish. His mother was born in New York and her parents were Austrian Immigrants. His father came from Russia when he was twelve. My father was raised in New York in an upper middle class home until the depression, which occurred just prior to my father's plans to go to college. He had to go to work and attend school at night. After a few years in the advertising office of the Hecht Company in Washington, he was hired by his eldest brother to work for him in an advertising agency in New York City. My father was talented and creative but, like my mother, fell victim to his eldest brother's point of view. He never really blossomed under the heavy hand of his eldest brother. Much of his daytime life was a secret to those of us who waited for him to come home at seven each night or, on the weekends, to emerge from his basement workshop or garden. Watching the TV show "Mad Men" has given me some insights into his work environment, as has reading letters that he wrote over his lifetime. So many of the letters to my mother were apologies. They were written with humor and clever drawings, but I am not sure with soul. I know he loved his two daughters and I think he loved his wife, but he had an internal battle and was somehow thwarted to express what could have been creative brilliance. The external battle was one my sister and I witnessed too often. My parents had yelling, door slamming arguments and then there was silence. Days of silence. I know, for me, the silence was the worst part.

Charles and Esther Harrison, wedding day July 1940

I was born in Takoma Park, Maryland in a Seventh Day Adventist Hospital because the hospital was vegetarian. My mother was sure, since they were vegetarians, that all the care would be better…maybe. She tried to nurse me and, even with her elder brother's constant coaxing, I was quickly switched to bottles and whatever went into commercial formula. So much for health!

By the time I was two, my father was offered the job from his brother and we moved to NYC. I do not any memory, photos or stories of two childhood kitchens: Washington DC and Manhattan. In fact, my parents shared very few family stories; nothing about the ancestors and where they came from, why they came to this country and what their lives were like. By the time my parents were born, each being the sixth of seven, everyone must have been tired of telling the stories.

Sisters: Lynn and Kathy in front of our house in Woodmere

Sisters a few years later: Kathy on the left and that is me in the hat.

My first kitchen memory is our apartment in Cedarhurst, Long Island, New York. We lived in a two-bedroom apartment, which seemed spacious until my sister was born when I was five and a half. My parents moved to the pullout couch in the living room so that the two girls did not have to share a room. That was foreshadowing of us having very separate lives. With almost six years between us, our experiences, except for dinnertime, were vastly different.

The kitchen, in this apartment, was a small room and I have few memories of that space or the food. My mother was not a great cook. She made rice, baked potatoes, salad and green beans. My dad ate his big meat meal at lunch with his clients. (Again, visions of that life reinforced by books, TV shows and the gossip I heard after he died about love affairs and poor money management). My earliest food memories are of going out to breakfast with my father on Sunday mornings and leaving my mother and sister at home. We had bacon and eggs and then had chewing gum to hide the smell of the bacon. It was a secret. I am pretty sure it was my only secret then, but now I know it was not my dad's!

When I was in the third grade, we moved to a rented cottage in Woodmere, also on Long Island. Cedarhurst and Woodmere are two of what is often referred to as the "Five Towns" ( Inwood, Lawrence, Cedarhurst, Woodmere, Hewlett). Our house had two bedrooms, living room, dining room and a small square kitchen at the back of the house that opened to a beautiful backyard. The attic was converted into two more bedrooms and a bath for my sister and me. There was little space in the kitchen to eat except to stand at the counter, which is where I ate breakfast. Most mornings I was up before my mother and sister and my dad would leave for work without eating, so I stood in the kitchen and ate my bowl of cereal in the peace and quiet. I did not mind. I also ate my favorite evening snack standing alone in the kitchen. When I was in seventh and eight grade I started babysitting and going out with friends. When I got home, even if it were 11 p.m. I would boil a pot of spaghetti, put it in a bowl with butter and ketchup and cheese and eat it quietly so that no one would know. I don't think I ever left any telltale signs, so no one did know. I am not even sure why I kept it a secret. My dad would have thought it funny and my mother would only care that I had not left a mess. I guess my dad sent the tone for food secrets and I do remember having others, like hiding candy bars between my mattress and box spring. So spaghetti cooking was another food secret. This was my first foray into cooking. I still think of it as comfort food—spaghetti, butter, ketchup and cheese!

When I was a freshman in high school, we moved to the third of the five towns: Hewlett. My parents bought their first home, a split-level house in a very elegant neighborhood. The kitchen was pink: wallpaper and cabinets. It was the first ceramic cooktop I had ever seen and I hated cooking on it. Our kitchen table had a wrought iron base and a marble top that had views from four windows of my father's breathtaking flower gardens. He perfected his craft of building furniture in our new basement and was a remarkable gardener. My mother got more involved with organizations that had to do with music and art, and played competitive tennis and bridge, but still was not much of a cook. We still ate baked potatoes, salad and green beans except when the cleaning lady came and she would cook something wonderful for my dad and me. My sister was not that interested in food and my mother was not straying from her vegetarian diet. So, once a week dad and I had chicken. I did do some cooking, but mostly for myself. My mother did not like the kitchen, or any part of the house, getting messed so my creativity was thwarted a bit. I am embarrassed to admit I inherited this trait from her—a source of frustration for my children but not my husband who is more compulsive about tidiness than I am. Despite the need to keep the kitchen neat, I did perfect my pasta sauce and it had no ketchup. Later on, my mother-in-law reintroduced ketchup cooking in her terrific stuffed cabbage.

By the time I left for college and had expanded my cooking a bit, I still knew nothing about baking, stews, meat or fish. It was mostly pasta and eggplant. But I was ready and excited to start on my own and was able to do some cooking (mostly Asian inspired) in a shared kitchen for two of my four years in college.

I started dating Joe the first day of my sophomore year of college. The second day of that school year, I called my boyfriend of three years at Harvard and ended our relationship. I knew that first date with Joe, where we talked and danced to music from a jukebox, that I had found my "soul mate" (sorry to be so corny). My heart was racing with what I knew was love. That next summer Joe was doing research at Woods Hole Marine Biological laboratories and I worked as a chambermaid in a B&B in the morning in exchange for an attic bedroom. He slept at the Marine Biological dorms, (remember this was the 60's). In the afternoon, I cleaned houses for researchers and their families. Believe it or not, it was a fabulous summer. I even got to clean the room of singer Judy Collins and met her father.

The next summer, we got married and we spent the summer at my parents home—Joe working as a lifeguard and I at a day camp. At the end of that summer, 1963, we rented a car and drove from New York to Buswell Street in Boston singing our favorite song:
*"We ain't got a barrel of money, we may be ragged and funny, but we will travel along, singing a song, side by side."*

# TWENTY-ONE KITCHENS
## A COOKBOOK MEMOIR

A galley kitchen in a furnished apartment or a grand space with all of the bells and whistles— the function is the same. It is food: the act of creating and the enjoyment of eating. It is the romance, the arguments, the whining child, the soothing cup of tea or the popping cork of champagne. It is dirty dishes and broken appliances. It is limited storage and too much stuff. It is no flour when you need to bake cookies for the second grade and it is praise and complaints. It is the center of domestic life.

I have had 21 kitchens since I was 20. The first two in Boston; one in Roxbury, Massachusetts; three in Minnesota; one in Kansas; three in Marblehead, Massachusetts; and two in Maine. Kitchen number 13 was in Greensboro, North Carolina and number 14 in Floyd, Virginia. A move to Kirkland, Washington and then to Nevada City, California; Penn Valley, California; Berkeley and, finally, Oakland brings the count to 19. The last two have been in Baltimore, Maryland. Six of these kitchens were brand new, some had a bit of remodeling or tweaking, and many were left untouched.

When I started to list all of my homes and remodels, I realized that the memories were more than the cabinets, counters and appliances. I have kept notebooks of recipes I've clipped from magazines and those that I invented or printed off of the Internet. These notebooks have become a diary. Part of the fun of looking back has been to see what has changed and what influenced these changes. But this is not just about kitchens and food. No matter who you are, life is rich with memories. These are some of mine.

## BOSTON 1963-1964

My first two kitchens were in an apartment building on Buswell Street in Boston. The building was owned by Boston University. It housed married students from the School of Theology. That year, the large five-story building had only two non-theology couples: one from the medical school (that was us) and one from the law school. Many of the theology students were from the then conservative south: not happy that Kennedy was president and feeling disconnected to the 60's liberal Boston political perspective. Most of us who lived in the cloistered academic world of the Northeast were as bewildered by their views as they were of ours. We were friends with one couple from the theology school. They were from Ohio and seemed to walk in both worlds with ease. This was 1963. I was 20, a civil rights advocate and caught under the spell of John F. Kennedy.

Our first apartment was a one-room furnished efficiency—no telephone, television or car. My contact with the outside world, when I wasn't in class or at work at Boston U Alumni office, was a small radio that I moved from the kitchen to the living/sleeping space. We slept on a hide-a–bed couch. When it was open the bed would hit the back of Joe's desk chair. He would often study into the wee hours of the morning, which forced me to learn to sleep with the light on. Today, when there is light from Joe's midnight reading, I wear an eye mask. Back in 1963, the light didn't bother me nor did slides of human brain sections being shown from a projector on the window shade. It never occurred to me to be freaked out by sharing our studio apartment with the full body skeleton that Joe kept next to his desk. All of these inconveniences added to my idea of adventure and I loved it. So many of my friends were living in fancy apartments with lots of new stuff. I took pride in our simple life. I was a real "snob" with foolish pride about trying to be different and thinking our simple life was better. This becomes a theme, but not necessarily a reality, for much of my life.

The kitchen was small and functional. There was enough room to store our few wedding gifts and a window that brought in city light. What came out of my first kitchen? Onion dip when guests came for a beer and spaghetti. Spaghetti with a rich thick tomato sauce, iceberg lettuce salads with grated cheese and croutons, and homemade chocolate cake.

I commuted to classes in Springfield, Massachusetts, 90 miles away, so that I could finish my coursework and start teaching. Three nights a week I slept at Joe's parents home where I was treated like the privileged daughter. His parents were both hard working, with little money to spare, but always generous. Joe was raised to get only A's in school, do housework and work in his father's drugstore. There was no time for extras. I tried to do some cooking and cleaning for the family and to be a companion to Joe's 12 year-old brother, Sandy. Joe's middle brother, Mark, was at college. Elsie and Leon seemed happy to have me and were very loving. It was obvious, though, that their first and only concern was that I not do anything to stop their son from becoming a doctor. (Including getting pregnant, which was their biggest fear).

My advisor at college knew that, even with all my efforts, I was still going to be three credits short to graduate a semester early. He came up with a generous plan that turned out to be more fun than work. He was writing his Ph.D. thesis and asked me to do research at the Rare Books Library at Harvard. The project took a total of about 10 hours.

I finished my coursework and the research and started my student teaching. My advisor arranged, again against school policy, for me to student-teach in Boston, so I no longer had to take the Peter Pan Bus, with no bathrooms, from Boston to Springfield. Just as I was writing this, a vivid memory came to me. It was a late Sunday afternoon and I was on the Peter Pan Bus to Springfield, along with many other college students heading to Springfield or Amherst. I was wearing a purple straight skirt and a matching sweater. I was sitting near the back of the bus next to a middle-aged woman who liked to talk. Halfway through the trip on the Massachusetts Turnpike, I knew if I didn't go to the bathroom I was going to be sitting in a wet skirt. I walked to the front of the bus and told the driver I was pregnant (years from that being true) and asked if he could stop at the next rest stop. The driver was reluctant but agreed to stop. What I didn't know was that when our bus stopped, the two other packed buses behind us had to stop. They all had to arrive at the same time. As I got off of the bus, a dozen other people decided to take advantage of the opportunity and raced to the restrooms. The bus drivers were not happy with me. My seat companion, however, was thrilled about my "pregnancy." I was distraught with my lie. I feared it would jinx me when I wanted to have a baby. It also brought back memories of my dad and the chewing gum lie. So I was physically comfortable but emotionally miserable. I would not miss those bus rides when the semester was over.

Spending three nights a week in Springfield required some planning. Joe would be too tired to cook and would have no time to shop. Each Sunday, I made three casseroles that just needed to be heated. I made something with hot dogs and green beans and, of course, tuna noodle casserole with canned mushroom soup and crispy onion rings. I also cooked cheap fatty lamb patties. I had to cook them with multiple preparation steps to get rid of all the fat. First I broiled them and threw out the grease. Then I baked them until no more fat was left and the patty was half of its original size. The final stage was to bake them with tomato sauce. They were really nothing more than hard disks with a slight lamb flavor, covered with sauce. The thought of them makes my stomach turn.

The smells from my apartment could not have been more interesting than onions and a little garlic and lots of tomatoes. My neighbor, however, had wonderful, rich, warm and lively aromas coming from their apartment, and the smells would fill the hallway. I didn't know what they were then but now, knowing more about food, I am sure they included cumin, coriander and cinnamon with a large dose of chili peppers. The aromas from my kitchen years later brought back memories of the smells that wafted from across the hall. I never met my neighbors, but I would sometimes see a woman from India in the laundry room. That fall semester, I was rarely home and there was little opportunity to meet neighbors except in the laundry room. I am not shy, and err on the side of being too friendly, but for some reason the opportunity to interact never felt right. Not just with her but with almost everyone. I know now that time in that building would have been richer if we had been able to make more friends. We knew two couples in the building: one from the law school who grew up in Springfield and Joe knew from high school, and the Denton's from Ohio. He was in the Divinity School and she was a teacher, and we were inseparable whenever there was an opportunity. We knew we were going to be moving in different directions and came from different beginnings, but there was something wonderful between us. We kept in touch for years mostly a yearly letter and one year a very special visit with us in Marblehead, Massachusetts.

So, if I did not know the smell of Indian Curry, what did I know of ethnic cooking? Little! My Asian housemate in college showed me some simple dishes and I had learned a few recipes from Eastern Europe, favored by Jewish immigrants, from my mother-in-law. My first attempt at one of Elsie's recipes was stuffed cabbage. I cooked the cabbage until all the leaves were soft and then started to make the sauce. The ground beef filling had been made earlier and safely stored in our little refrigerator. As I was getting the sauce ingredients together, I could hear my mother-in-law saying *"what about the ketchup?"* My mother-in-law's sweet and sour sauce was made with ketchup, Worcestershire Sauce and ginger snaps. Somehow making a sauce with ketchup didn't seem like cooking but not yet ready to ad lib, my sauce was ketchup based. The kitchen smelled heavenly. I assembled each roll with great care, two tablespoons of meat in each cabbage leaf and then rolled tightly. The next step was to pick from my many wedding gifts the ideal casserole dish. I had my eye on a red Dansk pot but loved a flowered one that had been put up on a high shelf. I got a chair and brought it down. The size was perfect. All the cabbage fit in a nice single layer with the sauce on top and bottom. Now all that was left was to cook the casserole and make some rice. Joe would be home in about an hour. I put the casserole on the stove on a slow simmer, got the rice started, and made some tea. I went into the living room to catch up on some reading when I heard what sounded like an explosion. It was. The casserole was glass and was never meant for stovetop cooking. There was cabbage and sauce on the ceiling, on the walls and on the floor. Everywhere that there was cabbage and sauce, there was also glass. As I stood frozen in the middle of this mess, I knew this was going to be the first of many cooking disasters, since I was a "seat of my pants" learner.

I remember every detail of the making of the stuffed cabbage, and the explosion, and the time it took me to clean up the mess with the radio blasting and my terrible voice trying to sing along. What I do not remember is what we had for dinner. I never remember going out to eat that first semester. Our lives were busy and money was very tight, so I am also sure that neither of us would have thought of take-out. Here is what I am guessing happened. Joe came home and found the whole thing funny and got me to find it funny. We then made some pasta or scrambled eggs and then probably took a walk. Life was so uncomplicated and our needs so small. You think when you are 20 that you have the power to always keep it that way, but you don't.

# ELSIE'S STUFFED CABBAGE

This is as close as I can get to what she made as she NEVER measured and it was never the same twice…my kind of cook!

| | |
|---|---|
| Cabbage | 1 large head |
| Tomatoes | 1 large can (I use a bit more as we like the sauce) |
| Beef | 2 lbs. lean ground beef |
| Onion | 2 chopped |
| Celery | 1 stalk finely chopped |
| Carrot | 1 finely diced |
| Ketchup | 1 cup |
| Worcestershire Sauce | a splash |
| Brown Sugar | hmm…depends on how sweet you like it. I go for about 1/2 cup. This might be too much for most people |
| Raisins | Handful (and this is defiantly optional…no raisins for my son) |
| Garlic | 1 clove smashed or finely diced |
| Ginger snaps | 1/2 lb. or more. Again, up to taste. The snaps add more sweetness and thicken the sauce. Of course, fresh ginger would be more sophisticated but not better. |
| Lemon | Juice of one lemon |
| Eggs | 2 |
| Rice | We always added a few handfuls of uncooked rice to the meat, but you can use breadcrumbs or just leave it all meat. |

1. Cut the core of the cabbage and boil in salted water for about 10 minutes or until the leaves separate. Drain and set aside.
2. Sauté 1 chopped onion until soft and then the celery and carrots.
3. Add the garlic, tomatoes, ketchup, lemon juice, brown sugar, ginger snaps and raisins (optional).
4. Taste for salt, pepper and sweet and sour. Too sweet, add some white vinegar or more lemon. Not sweet enough add sugar and ginger snaps.
   Worcestershire sauce is also a nice addition. Add a splash if you like.
5. Set the sauce aside.
6. Mix meat with the two beaten eggs, salt, pepper and a few handfuls of rice. Some cooks add more seasonings to the meat (garlic etc.).
7. Put a Tbsp. of meat inside each cabbage roll and roll up folding the sides in so it looks like a package.
8. Pour some of the sauce on the bottom of the baking pan and then place all the cabbage packets on top of the sauce. You may need more than one pan. Cover the top of the cabbage with the rest of the sauce
9. Bake 350 degrees until hot and the sauce is bubbling
   OR If you have a pan that can go on top of the stove, you can simmer the cabbage - DO NOT USE GLASS.

Fridays were my days to grocery shop, cook and clean, and listen to the radio. I had no classes and no work. One such Friday in November, my world went spinning out of control. It was on this day that President Kennedy was shot. If you are old enough to remember that day, then I am sure you remember where you were and what you did. I was alone. I had the radio on and was cleaning, sweeping, dusting and organizing our few possessions. I had bought a few flowers that morning and had put them on the table. No matter how tight our budget, I always found a way to buy flowers.

The music I was listening to was interrupted with the voice of the frantic newsman:

"The president has been hit by a sniper."

I am embarrassed to admit that at first I thought a snake had attacked the president. (viper?, sniper?) I thought that was odd and wondered how a snake got into his car. That silly moment lasted just that—a moment.

I sat on a chair by the window and listened to the radio, breathing heavy and whispering "oh no" until I could no longer control my tears. Sobbing and desperately trying to understand what was happening, I felt a great need to talk to someone. There was no way to reach Joe and all of my friends were at work. I guess it never occurred to me to call my parents. I would have had to use the public pay phone in the lobby. I stumbled down the four flights of stairs to the basement laundry room, crying but not yet frantic. The laundry room was the only common room in the building. There was one other person in the laundry room: a tall thin blonde graduate student doing his wash. I had seen him around, but we had never spoken. He was not the kind of person who would even nod at a fellow apartment building mate. He usually walked with his shoulders square and little expression. I could not control my sobbing as I asked:

" Have you heard the news?"

"No, what news?"

I told him that President Kennedy had been shot.

He said, "I'm not sorry" and walked out of the room.

Now I was frantic. I know the first thing I did after he walked out with his laundry basket was to sit (I was going to say collapse, but I just felt like collapsing, I was still in some control) onto the floor. A cold cement floor, surrounded by machines and no people was worse than my little apartment. I dragged myself up the four flights and sat by the radio until Joe came home.

We spent most of the next three days on campus. We would walk down our street and cross a small footbridge to be on the main campus where they had televisions installed in all the public rooms. There was little conversation, only stunned silence and quiet weeping and the occasional sound of coffee being sipped.

I know that the student with his hard heart could not have been the norm, but I will tell you this: the entire city of Boston was in such a state of grief that the air was heavy and dark even though the weather was clear. But in our little building, life seemed to be normal. Where was the grief for the loss of a life? Where was the sorrow that man is capable of such acts of violence? When does politics trump justice and respect for human life? The few of us who were in physical and emotional pain banded together, but nothing will ever erase my memory of the look of controlled joy on the face of that student, a future minister, the day Kennedy died.

It took a long time for life to get back to anything close to normal but we did have to go to work, go to school and eat and sleep. My Fridays were still at home alone. I walked to the local market, did laundry, without ever seeing that anti Kennedy resident again. One Friday, not too many weeks later, the stove died. I was pretty sure it was not from the cabbage volcano but a gas problem. I called the gas company and someone was coming within the hour. I didn't expect such prompt service and started to feel nervous. This was 1963, the year that the Boston Strangler was terrorizing the city. The MO was that most of his victims had some relationship to the medical profession. I was the wife of a medical student, so that put me on the "watch out" list. The "Boston Strangler," as he was called then and now, managed to gain access to his victims in their apartments. We had no security in our building and I was often home alone. It was a tense time. Now I was letting a strange man in my house. Sure he had on a gas company jacket, but anyone could get that. Maybe the Strangler worked for the gas company. That made sense. I reasoned that was how he got into all the apartments. So, I got my sewing scissors and held them open as he walked to my kitchen. I stood in the doorway with the scissors opened: alert and ready to ...do what? I guess stab him if he came towards me. He never laughed at me nor did he question what I was doing. I am sure during that period in Boston I wasn't the only nervous woman who thought she needed to defend herself against a kind and helpful gas repair man. When he was out the door and down the hall, I thanked him. He smiled back and went on his way, hopefully to be treated with a bit more dignity than I afforded him.

Midterms brought us some good news. I was finished with school and commuting. A graduate student and his wife moved out of their apartment, leaving a one bedroom unfurnished apartment available. I have no idea how we got to be the lucky couple to get this bigger apartment, but we were excited to pack our few things and move. The apartment not only had a bedroom, but it also had a real kitchen with a built in booth for "dining." It had two cabinets that divided the eating space from the cooking space. The cabinets had glass doors, and that was the beginning of my displaying pottery. It was all stuff we used every day but it was important that they were arranged in such a way that it said "a person with taste lives here" What is taste? My definition of it changes with each move. Each house brings out different sensibilities. I wonder if anyone thought I had bad taste. I see "taste" as a constant changing idea. My dark blue curtains were made from burlap, a twin bed pushed up against the wall served as our couch. This was the best we could afford and we thought it was great.

My life was getting busier. With classes completed, I had longer working hours at the Boston University Alumni office and was student teaching in a third grade in downtown Boston. The school was an inner city school when busing was still just an idea. I was in a third grade class and understood why I wanted to be a teacher. Despite the fact that my supervisor was cranky and some of the kids difficult, I loved it all. I became connected to one boy who I knew was intelligent but clearly had emotional and behavioral problems. He let me spend time with him as long as he could draw. There was so much to learn from his drawings and his sense of abandonment, but there was little I could do in ten weeks. It wasn't until years later that I knew that working with kids in need would be my vocation instead of teaching.

During this time, Joe was rarely home and I was busy, so I had little cooking inspiration. I did have a nice kitchen (no photos). The only thing I remember making that is worth mentioning is a many layered whipped cream cake for Joe's birthday. As I was bringing it to the folding bridge table (his parents were visiting), one layer started to slide and then they all slithered so that it was one big mess of whipped cream, berries and mushy angle food cake. We served it in bowls, ate it with a spoon and left none for the garbage.

Joe was born on George Washington's birthday, so I always made something with cherries until it started to feel silly. A dessert that I made for three years was something called "Washington Cherry Cake." This is not to be confused with the fruit and whipped cream cake that I made in 1963 that had to be eaten with a spoon. That cake was a store bought angel food cake cut in half with homemade whipped cream and cherries in the middle and on the top and sides. The Washington Cherry Cake is foolproof and you won't have the top sliding off into a gooey mess.

## WASHINGTON CHERRY CAKE

| | |
|---|---|
| Unflavored gelatin | 2 envelopes |
| Pitted sour cherries | 3 cans (16 oz.), packed in water |
| Sugar | 2/3 cup plus 1/4 cup |
| Lemon juice | 2 Tbsp. plus 1 Tbsp. |
| Almond extract | 1/2 tsp. |
| Heavy cream | 2 cups |
| Ladyfingers | 24 split (you might need more) |
| Cornstarch | 1 Tbsp. |
| Spring form pan 9" | |

1. Soften gelatin in 1/4 cup of cold water.
2. Drain juice from 2 cans cherries (1 1/2 cups).
3. Add sugar to juice and heat.
4. Add gelatin and stir until dissolved.
5. Add cherries from 2 cans, almond extract, and 2 Tbsp. lemon juice.
6. Chill mixture until set.
7. Whip cream.
8. Fold whipped cream into cherry gelatin.
9. Line the bottom and sides of spring form pan with ladyfingers.
10. Add half of cherry mixture. Cover with ladyfingers and then top with the rest of the cherry mixture.
11. Chill. While chilling, make the cherry topping.
12. Cherry Topping

    Drain juice from a third can of cherries.
    To the liquid add: 1/4 cup sugar, 1 Tbsp. lemon juice.
    Bring to a boil and stir in 2 Tbsp. cornstarch that has been diluted in a small amount of cold water. Stir until thick.
    Add cherries to thicken sauce. (The recipe calls for red food coloring. I never used that.)
13. When the cake is chilled and the topping cooled add, the topping to the top of the cake.

Another Friday I spent the afternoon with my friend Ellen whose future husband was a classmate of Joe's. She came to our apartment after her classes to talk about her wedding plans, and her fiancé was going to pick her up. Joe was in the kitchen, which was odd. Odd that he would be home so early and odd that he was cooking. He announced that he had made dinner and asked Ellen and Ricky to stay. I tried to hide my surprise. I felt if I made too big a deal out of his cooking he may not try it again and I was also too proud to let Ellen know that this was unusual. Of course, she knew us well and the charade was silly. So I went into the kitchen to see what was brewing and expecting to rave about the dinner we would have. One pot was filled with kasha, definitely enough for four. The second pot had one carrot, one onion and one potato.

We ordered pizza and we all got a good laugh at Joe's expense. I think he was hurt. He really thought he had made something wonderful. This would not be the last time Joe's feeling would be hurt by my laughing at his cooking. Being the strong willed person that he is, he now is quite a good cook and I have little opportunity to make fun of him!

Joe's impression of what we looked like in 1963

# ROXBURY, MASSACHUSETTS 1964-1967

(The door to the right of Joe's hooded head is ours. The curtains are my famous kitchen curtains.)

Our next stop was a brand new townhouse in a housing project in Roxbury. The St. Mark's Church and the Freedom House sponsored the construction of the project in the hopes of improving the quality of life for the residents in Roxbury and an attempt to integrate the community.

The St. Mark's Church was established in 1895 in Boston. In 1926, the church moved to Townsend Street in Roxbury and became the center of the social and political life of many black families who were moving to Roxbury. In 1961, St. Mark's Church was threatened to lose its home due to urban renewal. The church, not ready to give up without a fight, successfully raised money for a new concept in urban renewal. The church was allowed to remain and became nationally recognized for improving a blighted neighborhood. The church built a housing complex that was a cluster of townhouses for moderate-income families and set aside a percentage of homes for the very poor. The goal was not to ignore the poor but to make room for an emerging middle class. The Freedom House, a civil rights organization, joined forces with the church and added another criteria. The organization wanted it to be integrated. "Marksdale Gardens" was built for low and middle income black families with the hope of some non-black families moving in. We were that family! The first two years, we were the only white couple in the project. There was one mixed race couple, but the rest were black families who were thrilled, as were we, to be living in a wonderful new home.

Our new home had many benefits: two bedrooms, a small backyard and a sense of being part of something important. We were excited to be part of this small step in the civil rights movement and to get a beautiful two-bedroom house. The townhouse was two stories: downstairs was a big square kitchen. The living room had a sliding glass door that opened to a small patch of land for my first garden.

Upstairs were two bedrooms and a bathroom. Our family members donated furniture so all we needed were curtains. I grew up in a home where I never saw my mother thread a needle, so of course my next task was to teach myself how to sew and what better way to learn than to make curtains and drapes. I made drapes in a black and white toile for the sliding doors in the living room to coordinate with the faded black sectional couch. Some black and white throw pillows and a few red ones helped to connect with the large black, white and red braided rug that covered most of the floor. Some artwork, painted by family members, and some pine tables made by my father finished that room. We thought the room was a sure sign of good taste and ready for a magazine shoot. The kitchen needed little decorating. The turquoise appliances were standard issue and the white Formica counters and the light wood cabinets were all new and I was thrilled. There was a large window and an empty wall for a painting done by my mother-in-law and enough floor space for a kitchen table made by my dad. In keeping with our "colonial" theme, which was mostly because that is the only kind of furniture my dad knew how to build, I bought a Pennsylvania Dutch print fabric that had figures of a man and a woman with bits of turquoise flowers around the border. I spent hours cutting and hand-sewing those curtains. I did not have a sewing machine and would not get one until we moved to Minneapolis three years later. I made the top valance scalloped and the bottom curtain pleated. After two weeks of working on these, they were ready to be hung. I hung them, stepped back and cried. The top valance had all the figures upside down and there was no way to change it.

During these three years, I had many opportunities to explore how I felt about race, economic stratification and educational snobbery. I always thought I was void of prejudice, but every once in a while I was put to the test.

When we first moved to our new home, in what was once a Jewish neighborhood but now mostly Black, we asked one another some very probing questions about how we felt living in a neighborhood whose residents were Black:

"How would we feel if we were invited to someone's home for dinner?"

"How would we feel if no one invited us over? Would we make the first move?"

Those questions were easy to answer. We were comfortable asking our neighbors over, they were more hesitant to welcome us. Over the three years, some, but by no means all, of the neighbors became more and more trusting of us.

The next situation was one we did not anticipate and it took us some time to resolve. Occasionally, there would be loud noises outside of our bedroom window. It was most often on the weekends and it sounded like a small group of drunken folks. After numerous evenings where we were awakened and had done nothing for fear we would appear "racist," we finally said "the hell with walking on tiptoes. We live here and this is awful." So we opened the window and asked for them to please keep it down, as it was hard for us to sleep. It never happened again. We have had to deal with noisy, drunk neighbors in Berkeley and Baltimore and have gotten much more flack for complaining about the noise from white college students than we did from the group of black residents in Roxbury. We, of course, do not know what they thought of us and I am sure they were annoyed and maybe embarrassed, but we never had any evidence that it was held against us. There is no good way to tell people they are annoying you and it is especially hard when there are already built-in tensions. We knew that we were being watched and judged, but we also knew that the only way for it to work was for us to act as 'normal" as possible. Thinking back over the three years, this is the only negative interaction that I remember.

When friends outside our neighborhood asked, "How did we feel being the only white couple?" the answer seemed easy. I always said: "Great. No problem."

But how did I really feel living in a community of people whose life experiences were so different than mine? Day to day in our neighborhood was comfortable, but how did I really feel? One day I knew the answer, I think. I took the bus from Dudley Station in the middle of Roxbury at five p.m. and was heading home. I found a seat in the front of the bus behind the bus driver. The seat faced into the aisle. The bus filled up. By the time it was ready to leave the station there was no room to sit or stand. I started looking around the bus and realized that every other person was dark skinned. I looked at the people standing over me holding straps, I looked at those next to me, across from me and all the way in the back and then I looked at the driver. I then asked myself the question everyone else had been asking me: how did I feel? I took a moment to really give it serious consideration and then I knew that I felt fine! I must have smiled with the pleasure of that thought because, as I smiled, the gentleman holding the strap in front of me asked: "How do you feel?"

He had been watching me and must have read my mind.

I responded with my grin still fixed on my face: "Good, but I'm not sure how it would feel for you if the situation was reversed."

"Not as good I expect. Glad you like us." He smiled and that was the end of the conversation.

I often wondered what the people on the bus thought when they saw where I got off the bus, which stopped in the front of our housing project. Did they believe I lived there or that I was some social worker going to see a family?

Joe and I, already committed to civil rights, were getting more involved and signed up to travel to the South to support the activists working to improve voter registration. Joe had a few weeks vacation time that summer and I never worked in the summer, so this was how we planned to spend our free time. On June 21, 1964 James Chaney from Mississippi, Andrew Goodman and Michael Schwemer, from New York were shot and killed by the White Knights of the Ku Klux Klan. They had been working for " Freedom Summer", which is the organization we had joined. While attempting to register African Americans to vote the three young men were killed. We got scared and cancelled our plans. When I think back to that moment when we heard of their deaths, I remember how I felt. I was sad to know that these wonderful young men who were doing something that needed to be done were now dead. I was proud of us that we were planning to go south. I knew something like this could happen and now it had. We would not lose face because a lot of people were reconsidering. So we did not go! We did some things locally but I have always regretted that we were not brave enough to join many of our generation who really did make a difference. The deaths of Chaney, Goodman and Schwemer was the reason that the Civil Rights Act of 1964 and the Voting Rights Act of 1965 were passed.

My political point of view seemed to often spill over into my everyday life. Sometimes unintentionally, and sometimes because I let my feelings be known. Throughout my life I have not been afraid to share my views but I do try to make sure my audience is a receptive one. I don't want to get into a fruitless discussion where both sides feel strongly about their perspective. Although there have been times, maybe too many times, where I forget this rule and barrel ahead. While living in Roxbury and commuting to teach in an elementary school in Marshfield I worked hard at never engaging in political conversations. Roxbury and Marshfield were worlds apart and it was fun to be in both at the same time. Marshfield is a town on the south shore of Boston. In the 1960's it was mostly white, mostly Christian and definitely Republican. How do I know this?

The following two stories illustrate why I jumped to this conclusion. A few weeks into my first year the principal called me into his office. He handed me a slip of paper with dates while saying:

"I have arranged for a substitute for you for all these dates."

Dumbfounded and close to tears thinking I had done something wrong I asked:

"Why?"

He then explained that I was the first Jewish teacher in the system (how he knew I was Jewish was never discussed) and he had done research to learn the dates of the Jewish holidays. He wanted me to know that I could take them off. (This story is a dramatic contrast to a reverse experience many years later in Greensboro, North Carolina, but that comes later.)

I got my composure, thanked Mr. Thomas and told him that I would only need two days off. The rest of the dates I would be at work.

The Republican issue is of course easier to discover. You just have to look at the voting results after each election. But I had a more personal experience. In 1964, the staff at our school did a mock election. Goldwater got all the votes but one. Only one adult voted for Johnson. Now here's the thing that made it so obvious as to whom the lone democrat was. I was the only staff person who did not live in Marshfield. I was the only one who not only didn't live in town, but also lived in Roxbury. Most everyone knew I grew up in New York and yes; there was the Jewish thing. So who was the Democrat in the crowd was a no-brainer.

For the three years I worked in Marshfield, I never once felt that I was being treated unfairly or without respect. I was included in conversations in the teacher's room and felt very much a part of the faculty. But that is where it ended. No one was really my friend. Once a month, the faculty had to stay at the school from six until nine in the evening so parents could come for conferences. It was a great idea except for one small problem that only impacted me. Everyone living nearby went home at four and came back at six. It was way too long a drive for me to do that. I was never invited to anyone's home for dinner. I sat in the building by myself, ate my sandwich and fussed with papers on my desk. They just never thought about what I was doing those afternoons and I never let on that I felt isolated. I wonder how much of that was my fault. Was I just as happy not to get closer to my colleagues? Our lives outside of work were so different. Was I protecting my privacy? Was I just trying to avoid having to explain myself or defend my point of view? I cannot answer those questions because I am so different now. I never leave a coffee shop or a bus or train without having a conversation with someone. I think in my 20s I was more cautious and wanted my work life to be smooth and uncomplicated. I am sure I never gave anyone any clues that I wanted friendships. Would my work life have been different and would I have liked it better? I don't think so. There seems to have been a pattern in my 20s and, as I write this, perhaps, in my childhood as well. I was not a joiner of social groups, sororities, clubs, etc. I still am not drawn to that kind of socializing, but I love conversations, just smaller groups.

I worked until my pregnancy was evident. It was school policy that you could not teach while pregnant. The funny thing was that many of my students knew long before the staff noticed. One of my fourth graders told another teacher that he thought I was pregnant. He laughed at the student and then came to tell me the "funny story." I couldn't lie and told him it was true. He gave me a hug and promised not to tell but I couldn't put him in that position. I also didn't know what other people the student was telling. I made an appointment with the principal. He was really nice about it and seemed genuinely sorry that I had to resign. It was the policy of the town and no one wanted to risk breaking the rules. Two weeks later was the end of my teaching career in Marshfield. This policy would seem shocking today to working women, but in 1966 Marshfield's policy was not that far off the norm. The strict rules included a dress code. Even though I worked with young children, I was required to wear dress shoes, preferably with a heel, and absolutely no pants. I kept a pair of flat comfy shoes under my desk and put my heels on when I went out into the hall. There were times when I would forget to change and if the principal caught me, he would give me that sly smile that said he was going to pretend he didn't see me. He knew most of the women wore flats in the classroom and let us get away with that, but in the halls it did put him in an awkward position. Who knew if a parent might be in the building? So pregnant, a much bigger "no no' than the dress code, meant that in the beginning of my fifth month, my career was over and I would not have a job again until we move to Marblehead, Massachusetts in 1973. From November 1966 (Jon was born in March, a month premature) to September 1973, I was a stay-at-home mom with the exception of a small part time job in Kansas while the kids were in school.

Joe took this photo while we were visiting my family in New York. We are about to go out. I am pregnant and unemployed!

Starting in 1964, I became an avid Julia Child fan, reading and cooking from *Mastering the Art of French Cooking* and faithfully watching her on television. Every week I would make a Julia Child recipe, all the time staring at my upside down curtains in my turquoise kitchen. I also cooked many of the recipes from the *New York Times*. One Sunday, there was a recipe for something called "cannelloni." I bought all the ingredients, including chicken that I shredded and flavored with nutmeg. After the filling was made, I started to make what I thought was going to be a pastry dough. I mixed the flour and eggs and started to knead. I remember thinking it was like kneading a rubber band. The dough was rolled and cut into squares. All of this was out of my frame of reference. The next step was to boil water and drop the squares into the boiling water. Then it hit me. I screeched: " I just made noodles!" Joe came racing from the study to see what I was screaming about. I still have that recipe on the original faded newspaper. I haven't made this recipe in years but writing about it inspires me.

# CANNELLONI

This is the recipe that became my first noodle-making experience. I have set up the recipe so that the noodle making is more evident and have adjusted some of the ingredients to match how I made it after the first attempt.

| | |
|---|---|
| Chicken | 1 3 1/2 lb. |
| Celery | 1 stalk |
| Carrot | 1 cut in quarters |
| Parsley | 1 bunch |
| Butter | 5 Tbsp. |
| Flour | 1 1/2 cup plus 5 Tbsp. |
| Milk | 1/2 cups |
| Heavy cream | 1 cup |
| Swiss cheese | 1 cup grated |
| Parmesan cheese | 2 cups grated |
| Mushrooms | 1/2 lbs. finely chopped |
| Shallots | 2 Tbsps. chopped |
| Olive oil | 1 Tbsp. |
| Onion | 2 cups chopped |
| Garlic | 1 clove minced |
| Thyme | 1/2 tsp. |
| Bay leaf | 1 |
| Basil | 1 tsp. dried |
| Tomatoes | 4 peeled and chopped |
| Tomato paste | 2 Tbsp. |
| Sugar | 1/2 tsp. |
| Nutmeg | 1/2 tsp. |

PROCEDURE:

CHICKEN:
   1 Combine the chicken with the celery, carrot, a few sprigs of parsley and peppercorns in an enough water to cover the chicken.
   2. Simmer until the chicken is done. Cool the chicken in the broth.
   3. Remove the skin and bones from the chicken. The recipe suggests grinding the meat. I shred it. I like the texture.
   4. Add 1/2 tsp. nutmeg and 1/2 cup chopped parsley. Refrigerate while you prepare the rest of the steps.

MUSHROOM SAUCE:
1. Melt 4Tbsp. butter in a saucepan. Add the chopped shallots. Cook briefly. Add the chopped mushrooms and cook until they wilt and the liquid is evaporated.
2. Sprinkle with 5 Tbsp. flour and then add the milk and cream.
3. Cook the sauce until it is thick and remove from the heat.
4. Add 1 cup Swiss cheese, salt and pepper to taste and set aside.

TOMATO SAUCE:
1. Heat 1Tbsp. of butter with 1Tbsp. olive oil in a saucepan.
2. Add the onions and garlic and cook until the onions wilt.
3. Add 1/2 tsp. thyme, 1 bay leaf, 1 tsp. basil, the 4 chopped tomatoes, tomato paste and
4. 1/2 tsp. sugar.
5. Cook until the sauce thickens. It should yield about 3 cups.
6. Set the sauce aside.

PASTA:
1. Place 1 1/2 cups of flour on a board and make a well in the center.
2. Break 2 eggs into the depression in the flour.
3. With your hands work the eggs and flour together until it forms a ball.
4. Knead the dough until it is smooth and elastic up 5. Cover the dough with a towel and let it sit for 1 hour.
6. Roll half the dough out on a lightly floured board until it is transparent. Cut the dough into squares that are 4 by 4 inches. Roll out the remaining dough and cut it to 4 " squares.
7. Drop the squares into boiling water (use a large pasta pot) for 2 to 3 minutes. Drain the squares on a flat surface.

ASSEMBLY:
1. Add 1/2 of the mushroom sauce to the chicken.
2. Add 1/2 of the tomato sauce to 1/2 of the mushroom sauce. Mix well.
3. Put equal amount of chicken-mushroom filling along the bottom end of each square. Roll the pasta to enclose the filling. It will look like a filled tube.
4. Spoon mushroom-tomato sauce on the bottom of a baking dish large enough to hold the pasta.
5. Arrange the cannelloni in a single layer on top of the sauce and then cover with the remaining mushroom-tomato sauce.
6. Sprinkle with 1/2 cup Parmesan cheese.
7. Bake at 350 degrees for 30 minutes (longer if the ingredients have been refrigerated) Dish can be assembled in advance.
8. Serve with the remaining tomato sauce and Parmesan cheese.

It is a lot of work. I suggest you do all the parts the day before because you still have to make a salad and dessert.

Our three years in Roxbury were, in many ways, idyllic. Yes, Joe worked long and hard hours and was studying all the time. My job, teaching in Marshfield and commuting an hour each way, made my weekdays long but somehow we seemed to have time for friends. There were many dinner parties and sometimes a movie, although movies were rare because it was an expensive way for Joe to take a nap.

My first cookbook was a small navy paperback with a spiral spine. The title: *Second Helpings* by Marian Burros and Lois Levine is a perfect diary of what was the fashion in food in 1963. Food with titles such as "Bacon and Cheese Canapés," "Blue Cheese and Almond Spread," "Chinese Beef" and" Chicken and Grapes." But this little cookbook was more than food now long out of fashion. It introduced many new cooks to Fondue, Pâté de Maison, Arangini Siciliani, Chicken Kiev and Lobster Savannah. What it did for me was make me famous in our small circle of friends. Everyone was served "Beef Roulades" at least once and many, even today, 50 years later, ask " remember that fabulous crepe and beef thing you use to make."

This recipe was the dish I made and I am not changing one word of it from its original printing in the wonderful treasure of a cookbook *Second Helpings* Thank you, Marian and Lois, for starting me on the road to loving being in the kitchen, even when I had to stare at ugly curtains.

# BEEF ROULADES

BATTER:
- Mix and sift
  - 1 cup flour-sifted
  - 1 Tbsp. sugar
  - dash of salt
  - 3 eggs: beat and add to dry ingredients
  - Add   1 cup of milk
  - Add   2 Tbsp. melted butter

Strain through a fine sieve. Let stand 3 hours or more—overnight. Wipe heated 6" or 7" fry pan with buttered wax paper. Pour in about 3 Tbsp. batter, pouring off excess. When set and brown on underside, turn and brown on other side. Repeat entire process making at least 8 large, very thin pancakes. FILLING:

Brown
- 3/4 lb. ground chuck, round etc.
- 1 medium onion finely chopped
- 1/2 lb. mushrooms, finely chopped
- In 2 Tbsps. Butter

Add
- 1/2 tsp. salt
- dash pepper
- 1 tsp. dry mustard
- 1 garlic cloves, minced

Simmer 5 minutes. Add
- 1/2 cup ketchup
- 1 Tbsp. bottled steak sauce
- 1 tsp. parsley, snipped
- 1 tsp. oregano
- 1/4 tsp. rosemary
- 1 bay leaf, crumbled
- 2 cups cheddar cheese, coarsely crumbled
- 1/2 cup parmesan cheese, shredded

Cover and simmer until cheese is almost all melted. Remove from heat. Spread beef mixture on pancakes. Fold in two sides and roll up. Place in greased baking dish. Sprinkle with
- 1/2 cup parmesan cheese, shredded
- 16 slices mozzarella cheese - place 2 on each roll
- paprika

Refrigerate or freeze. When ready to serve, pour over 1/2 cup dry sherry.
Bake in 350 degree for 30 minutes. Mozzarella should be melted and browned.
My notes: you can ease up on the cheese but do not change the seasonings. They really work to make this dish a true 1960's showstopper

One special dinner party was our first occasion to entertain a real grown-up who was not family. Joe was fond of his attending physician at Samuel Shattuck Hospital. He was an engaging, intelligent physician from Argentina. We invited the rest of Joe's medical school team and their wives along with Dr. Erneste and his wife. I went to work researching the food of Argentina. This required a trip to the library and finding little more than beef and avocado recipes and some discussions of spices.

I made a spicy guacamole and a platter of assorted salamis and cheeses for appetizers. The dinner was beef tenderloin seasoned with horseradish. I also made eggplant and rice. Pie for dessert. Not really Argentinian food, but the best I could do. The evening got off to a shaky start. The doctor and his wife arrived late. The rest of us, three other couples, did not want to start eating or drinking until they came. It was nerve wracking. None of us had entertained an attending physician. When they finally arrived, they turned down my margaritas and requested martinis. Oops. Joe, a few years later, would have been well prepared, as that became his drink of choice, but that evening we had no idea how to make one and had none of the ingredients. They drank some wine. Neither of them touched the avocado but enjoyed the salami and cheese. The dinner conversation was lively and they seemed to enjoy themselves, probably because we were all fawning over them and made them the center of our attention. Our friends were good sports but it was a long time before we invited an attending physician for dinner again. Their level of sophistication outclassed us.

Joe continued to enjoy working with Dr. Erneste and didn't mind the long hours. I got used to Joe not coming home for dinner and sometimes not coming home at all if there was an evening emergency. One such night was Tuesday November 9, 1965. I got home from work around 4:30 p.m., turned on the radio and decided that the freezer compartment of the refrigerator was so encrusted with ice that it was crucial that it be defrosted. I got to work with a small chisel, trying to dislodge ice blocks. At 5:15 I lost all electrical power. What had I done? I was sure I hit some electric line that blew the fuse. I made my way to the front door to get help from my neighbor and noticed that the entire project was dark. No one had lights. Had I hit some central power line? What had I done? Well, of course, it wasn't my fault but I sure thought so. A neighbor had a transistor radio and we all learned, much to our shock, that the entire Eastern Seaboard was without power. It was The Blackout! This became a moment in time were the neighbors came together in a shared experience. Many of our neighbors were friendly, some were our friends and others were not sure about the "white couple," but that night we were all family.

After our second year, two more housing projects were built in the neighborhood and two fellow medical student couples moved into them. The black residents were as curious about us as we were of them. The integration idea was slow in happening. In this first project, we were the only white couple. After the awkward adjustment and testing period, we became very close with a few families. One favorite friend's home was where I parked my light green VW "bug." Many an evening when I got home from work, I would be invited in for tea. My friend and her husband had a young daughter whom I remember loved to dance. Graceful and not shy, she was a pleasure to watch. I don't know anything about them now, as we have not kept in touch. I was young and didn't collect people the way I do now. I do not want anyone who walks into my life to leave even if we live on different coasts. When we left Roxbury three years later, we left all that was important to us behind. We did just what our neighbors thought would happen. We were about to be upwardly mobile.

Our last year in Roxbury, one of the other medical student couples was going to have a baby. She was the first in the medical school class to have a baby. I was in my first trimester and would be the second in the group to give birth. Needless to say, we had to give Holly a wonderful shower. Joyce, the other medical student wife in Roxbury, and I co-hosted a Ladies Luncheon. The menu had to be unique. Artichokes were our first thought. It was a new item for many (not me—another thing my mother knew how to make), just starting to show up on the East Coast but not exactly what we had in mind. Joyce, with a look of excitement asked, "Have you read about quiches in Julia Child's cookbook?" Well I had but I didn't remember thinking much of it. It may have been one of the few recipes I had ignored. Joyce said she had tasted Quiche Lorraine and it was divine. We were both sure no one would have heard of it so we grabbed our cookbooks and made a plan. We would make four Quiche Lorraines, but added "fromage de gruyere", Swiss cheese. This was a combination of the first two quiche recipes in *Mastering the Art of French Cooking*. The tarts had a wonderful buttery crust filled with bacon, eggs, cream, nutmeg and Swiss cheese. There isn't one ingredient in that dish except the nutmeg that is on my diet today. Those quiches were packed with fat, no wonder they were fabulous. We included a green salad, of course none of the wonderful greens we have today were available then, but I know we didn't use iceberg lettuce. That was for tacos. I have tried to remember the dessert but the memory is gone. Joyce and I both liked to bake so I am sure it was a delicious, rich something that took forever to make. We set the tables with white tablecloths, big bouquets of spring flowers, and wine for everyone but Holly and me. We were cramped in the small townhouse, but it was joyous.

Halfway through the afternoon, something struck me. Joyce, Holly and I (the two hosts and the guest of honor) all lived in "black" neighborhoods. All our neighbors were black. Much of our day-to-day life was with our black neighbors and yet, there was not one black person at this celebration. Everyone that day was white, young and the wife of a medical student. At 25 years old, I was still not exactly who I wanted to be.

Before I leave Boston I must include some recipes that bring back memories of time and place. Not knowing a lot about fish, my first attempt was a filet of sole. I loved it, however my future sister-in-law did not, but never said a word. I served it to her not knowing she "hated" fish. I also overdid the mushrooms. Serving mushroom turnovers with the fish was a bit redundant. I redeemed myself with a terrific cheesecake.

# FILLET OF SOLE WITH MUSHROOMS

We did not eat a lot of fresh fish in the 1960's; now fish is the mainstay of our diet. This was one of the few fish dishes that I made. Fresh fish is so wonderful that I would now never think of adding a heavy cream sauce. Try this without the cream and add herbs.

| | |
|---|---|
| Mushrooms | 1 lb. clean, remove stems and slice |
| Shallots | 1 Tbsp. chopped |
| Lemon juice | 3 Tbsp. |
| Dry white wine | 3/4 cup |
| Olive oil | 2 Tbsp. |
| Butter | 8 Tbsp. |
| Heavy cream | 2/3 cup |
| Four | 4 Tbsp. |
| Fish: sole or flounder | 3 lbs. |
| Salt and pepper | |

PROCEDURE:

1. Melt 2 Tbsp. of butter and 1 Tbsp. olive oil in large skillet. Add the mushrooms, cook for 2 minutes.
2. Add the shallots and cook another 2 minutes.
3. Add 2 tsp. of lemon juice.
4. Butter a shallow "cook and serve" dish that can be used on top of the stove. Lay the fish fillets side by side. Fold if you need to.
5. Pour in the wine and enough water to come to the top of the fish and bring to a slow simmer on top of the stove until liquid is hot. Cover and cook until fish flakes (about 8 minutes total).
6. In a heavy saucepan, melt 4 Tbsp. of butter and stir in the flour.
7. Add lemon juice, salt and pepper.
8. Add the mushroom caps and pour on top of the fish.
9. Serve with rice and a green vegetable.
10. Add some of the poaching liquid and heat, stirring with a whisk until it is thick. Gradually add the cream until it is thickened.

# MUSHROOM TURNOVERS

| | |
|---|---|
| Cream cheese | 9 oz. |
| Butter | 1/2 cup plus 3 Tbsp. |
| Flour | 1/2 cup plus 2 Tbsp. |
| Onion | 1 chopped |
| Mushrooms | 1/2 lb. fine chopped |
| Sour cream | 1/4 cup |
| Thyme | 1/4 tsp. |
| Salt and pepper | |

PROCEDURE:
1. Cream cheese and butter should be at room temperature.
2. Mix the butter and cream cheese together. Slowly add the flour and knead until smooth.
3. Chill for 1/2 hour.
4. Preheat oven 350 degrees.
5. Roll dough to 1/8" thick and cut into 3" rounds.
6. Place 1 tsp. of filling in the dough rounds. Fold dough in half over the filling and pinch the edges together. Prick with a fork to seal.

Filling:
1. Sauté onions in 3 Tbsp. of butter.
2. Add the mushroom and cook until liquid is gone.
3. Season and sprinkle with flour.
4. Stir in the sour cream and cook gently until thick.

# ORANGE CHEESECAKE

| | |
|---|---|
| Flour | 1 cup plus 3 Tbsp. |
| Sugar | 2 1/4 cups |
| Orange rind | 2 Tbsp. grated |
| Butter | 1/2 cup |
| Eggs | 5 eggs plus 3 yolks |
| Vanilla extract | 1 tsp. |
| Cream cheese | 2 1/2 lbs. |
| Heavy cream | 1/4 cup |
| Orange juice | 1 cup |
| Cornstarch | 2 Tbsp. |
| Orange | 1 |

PROCEDURE:

Crust:
1. Combine 1-cup flour, 1/4 cup sugar and 1 Tbsp. grated orange rind.
2. Cut in 1/2-cup butter until the mixture is crumbly.
3. Add 1 egg yolk and 1/2 tsp. vanilla and blend thoroughly.
4. Pat 1/3 dough on bottom on 9" spring form pan.
5. Bake 400 degrees. for 8 to 10 minutes. Cool.
6. Butter sides of pan and slip in bottom. Pat the remaining dough evenly around the sides up to about 2 1/4" from the bottom. Chill.

Filling:
1. Have the cream cheese at room temperature.
2. Combine cream cheese with 3Tbsp. flour, 1 3/4 cups sugar and 1Tbsp. grated orange rind, a dash of salt and 1/2 tsp. of vanilla.
3. Blend well on medium speed of mixer.
4. Add 5 eggs plus two yolks, one at a time, blending well.
5. Stir in 1/4cup heavy cream.
6. Pour into crust.
7. Bake 500 degrees 8 to 10 minutes and then reduce the heat to 225 degrees for 1 hour and 20 minutes.
8. Turn the oven off and let it stand for 10 minutes.
9. Remove from oven and cool in pan.
10. Chill several hours or overnight.
11. Cover with 1/2 of orange glaze.
12. Dip orange sections in the remaining glaze and arrange on top of cake.

Glaze:
1. Combine 1 cup orange juice with 1/4 cup of sugar, dash of salt.
2. Bring mixture to the boil and blend in 2Tbsp. cornstarch that has been diluted in a small amount of cold water.

Stir into mixture and cook until thick.

# MINNEAPOLIS 1967-1971
## St. Louis Park

Our apartment is the lowest floor to the right of the front door. The light blue drapes are mine. Taste? They match the building's front door. I never noticed that until I looked carefully at this photo. Note tree is in full spring bloom and snow is on the ground.

Joe graduated from medical school. Our next stop was his medical internship and residency in hematology and oncology at the University of Minnesota. We drove from Boston to Minneapolis with our two-month-old son, Jonathan. Packing the VW and saying good-bye to family and friends was not easy. They were horrified that we would go so far away with a new baby. Joe's mother was sure, until the last minute, that we would make another plan. That never occurred to us. It was a great academic opportunity for Joe and I was ready for the adventure. I was to be a stay-at-home mom and I was young enough to be sure it would be great. Jonathan was a tiny infant (born a month early) and the three-day drive was a challenge, but somehow nothing was deterring our excitement. Our apartment was leased sight unseen and the neighborhood picked by a friend of my father's. It was a lovely neighborhood filled with three story apartments and trees but not near anything to walk to and a long drive to the hospital. It was a two-bedroom garden apartment in St. Louis Park. Calling a ground level apartment "garden" in Minneapolis is laughable. The year we lived there, we could not see out of the windows from the end of October until early April: SNOW. That is all we saw. Beautiful white snow and then dirty snow. I had no car. Joe had to have the car, as there was no public transportation. I was alone with an infant and no family or friends. I will admit that I started to have second thoughts but refused to admit to our families that, perhaps, we had made a mistake.

St. Louis Park Apartment. Galley kitchen. Feeding Jonathan. (Why Joe just took a photo of me feeding Jon without showing Jon was silly but this is the only photo that shows a bit of the kitchen. All our other photos are of Jonathan crawling, sitting and sleeping.)

At this time in my life I had few interests beyond cooking and reading. My next-door neighbor, who was childless and didn't work, was available during Jon's nap times. I suggested Scrabble and she agreed, as long as she could also watch her soap opera. The arrangement seemed doable. I think I would have done anything to be with another human who knew how to talk. I would have my back to the TV, and she would face the TV so she could watch and play Scrabble. I had never seen a soap opera. The one that was on during our hour together was "Days of Our Lives." Here is what happened: I got hooked. After a while, we stopped playing Scrabble and just drank tea and watched television. I know it does not sound very exciting or stimulating, but the alternative was worse.

Having one car, with Joe on call every other night and every other weekend, was not working for me. Soap operas were fun for an hour but I needed more. I don't even remember doing much cooking in that apartment. The kitchen was fine, an ordinary galley but Joe had no time or energy for socializing and I only cooked what we needed to sustain ourselves. It was a long, cold and lonely year for Jonathan and his mom. I was spending too much time thinking about and worrying about all that could go wrong with Jonathan. Although premature, he was developing on or before schedule and was perfectly normal. I just had nothing else to do but be involved with his development and happiness…most of the time. Sometimes I screwed up on the mother thing. One afternoon, Jon was in his crib napping and my Scrabble/TV partner was not visiting. I was in the living room reading a book when, much to my horror, a mouse ran across the living room floor. Maternal instincts, well, not too evident at that moment. I ran out of the apartment and, when the door closed, it locked and my sleeping son was alone with a mouse on the loose. Thank goodness the manager was home and I got back into the apartment before Jon woke. The mouse had time to escape to another apartment. I have no idea what I would have done had the manager been out. Thinking about it now, I guess I would have found some neighbor at home and called the police to come break down the door. Whew, that is a scary thought. I am so glad I never had to go that far. When we moved to Leavenworth Kansas I redeemed myself. I befriended a mouse that lived in our kitchen for a few weeks and never once ran out of our home leaving a helpless child alone. At least I don't remember doing that again. I have no intention of checking with my children to see if they have any memories of abandonment. I don't want to know.

My life wasn't filled with a lot of stimulation but I did have a few friends other than my Scrabble partner. There were two other couples in an apartment complex, a few blocks away. They were married to residents so the horrible internship year was behind them. They too had young children. One summer day, Bettina and I were going to take the kids (she had two) and go to a park. Before we were going, I was giving Jon lunch in the hopes that he would nap in the stroller. We were both dressed and ready to go as soon as he was finished eating. He was still very young and was in an infant seat on the floor joyfully kicking his feet waiting to eat. I did use baby food from a jar as often as I made "homemade," and had no qualms about creating a lunch that was little more then opening the jar and stirring. That day it seems my food supply was low and all that was there were some beets. Jon had yet to try beets, but he was a good eater and easy to please. I sat on the floor with him and put the first big spoonful of beets in his mouth. He seemed surprised at the taste and then made an interesting communication decision. He spit the entire mouthful of red beets with perfect aim, all over the front of my very white sundress! Now he was crying with hunger and I was frantic to make something for him to eat and to change my clothes and in the midst of all this Bettina arrived. My chaos made her day. She never stopped laughing and her good humor became contagious. It was a great day.

My friendship with Bettina was interesting. I got to know her because she also grew up in the Five Towns on Long Island. A mutual friend of our parents put us together. She was beautiful, a bit older and pleasant company, but we never got very close. Her husband was a surgical resident and they moved in a world different from ours, but that first year she was another center to my sanity. Without her, I think I really would have gone stir crazy. In fact, even with her I did act a bit nuts.

There was the night that Joe called saying he was about to leave the hospital and would be home in a half hour. Remember, this is way before cell phones. An hour passed, then another hour and no Joe. I called the police and then I called Bettina. I didn't want to be alone when the police called back telling me that Joe had been in an awful car accident. I was sure that was what I would learn. The police assured me that there had been no reports of accidents that evening. Hours later Joe came home, looking exhausted and shocked to see me upset. What happened, and had happened before and would happen again, was that he got paged as he was preparing to leave. The expectations in those days for interns were: you get paged, you go! He got so involved with an emergency room crisis that he forgot that I was expecting him and that I was a "class A" worrier. There was no doubt in either of our minds, it was time to move closer to the hospital. Real close.

With the year's lease up, we found the perfect new home.

Melbourne Street, Minneapolis

We moved to "Dinkytown," a University of Minnesota neighborhood filled with small apartments and big old homes. We rented a house whose previous tenants must have been party-loving students who had little regard for house maintenance. It was fun bringing that house to life. Joe started what would be a long lasting hobby as a woodworker and built us a terrific worktable in the kitchen. We painted it yellow with big abstract flowers on the side panels. Probably tacky but we loved it. Now I had all the space I needed to roll piecrusts, make everyone's favorite noodle kugel and keep on practicing my French cooking. Our second child, Wendy, was born while we lived in this house and we felt like a real family. The kitchen was old, the appliances typical of a rental, but that room was the center of our lives. It is odd that I have no photos of that kitchen, just lots of memories.

It was while living in this house that Joe's hours eased up a bit; at least enough so that we could occasionally have some social life. Entertaining was often casual and last minute and the winters were cold and long, so soup became a welcomed stand by.

## SOUPE AU PISTOU
### A popular winter Minnesota supper

This is a traditional vegetable soup and you can use any vegetables that are in season or are your preference. I love parsnips so my soup will usually have parsnips. What makes this soup my favorite is the pistou. Today I use more tomato and lots of pistou. It does seem to add more depth and flavor when you add the pistou at the end. The basil seems to loose its punch if it cooks too long. The soup does freeze well.

|  |  |
|---|---|
| Dry white beans | 1/4 cup (easy alternative - use good quality canned beans) |
| Onions | 1 cup, diced |
| Tomatoes | 1 lb., peeled, seeded and coarse chopped (1 1/2 c) |
| Carrots | 1 1/2 cup, diced |
| Potatoes | 1 1/2 cup, diced |
| Leeks | 1 cup, coarsely chopped |
| Green beans | 1 1/2 cup, sliced |
| Zucchini | 1 1/2 cup, diced (do not peel) |
| Celery Leaves | 1/2 cup, chopped |
| Pasta | 1/2 cup small, shaped pasta |
| Saffron threads | 2 pinches |
| Olive oil | 6 Tbsp. |
| Garlic | 5 cloves (or to taste) |
| Basil | 1/2 cup fresh, 5 Tbsp. dried |
| Tomato paste | 2 Tbsp. |
| Parmesan cheese | 2 cups |

PROCEDURE:

1. Cook the dry beans in 3 cups of water until tender. Save the cooking liquid. If using can beans, you will have to adjust the water of soup.
2. In heavy soup pot, heat 4 Tbsp. of olive oil. Stir in onions, cook until soft.
3. Add the tomatoes and cook for 3 to 4 minutes.
4. Add 3 quarts of water and bring to boil over high heat.
5. Add vegetables and saffron and simmer uncovered until they are tender.
6. Add pasta and cook until soft but not gummy.
7. Make the pistou while soup is cooking.
	In a blender or mortar and pestle, mix the garlic, basil, 6 Tbsp.
	of olive oil, tomato paste and 1/2 cup of cheese together.
8. Stir the pistou into the soup and serve with the remaining cheese and bread.

Life in our new home was a dramatic change from our apartment in St. Louis Park. I had a real home with three bedrooms, a living room, a dining room, a basement and a yard big enough for a sand box and some flowers. To the left of our house was a four unit complex. In one of the units lived a university faculty husband, his wife and their young son who was the same age as Jon. They were intellectuals, interesting and the mother needed a friend as much as I did. Our boys became toddlers together. My days were already better but shortly my world got even larger. One block down the street I met another mother with a son the same age and we were really kindred spirits. A short drive away was yet another mom, the wife of a cardiology resident in Joe's year, who also had a son the same age.

Joe didn't need the car because it was an easy walk to the hospital. Since he slept at the hospital every other night, Jonathan and I had lots of time to explore the city. But the truth is that there was so much to walk to that we only used the car for shopping or outings too far away. No more daytime television and lots more cooking. I was out of the doldrums and excited to be pregnant with our second child.

Jonathan and Wendy are 24 months apart and I thought we were brilliant in our planning…until they were two and four. That was a challenging year. But a two year old and a newborn were perfect. Jon was toilet- trained and still an easy child. Wendy, as with all newborns, needed lots of attention, but Jon was happy to sit next to me and look at books while I nursed his new sister. Two years later, the dynamics were less peaceful!

Because we lived so near the hospital, we discovered that there was a world outside work and childcare. But mostly we made friends with people who had young children, and our social life was mostly with the kids. Joe built a small child-sized red table with two red benches so that, when we had guests all the two and three year olds had their own party.

Food for those occasions was often soups, stews, pasta, hamburgers and hot dogs. We wouldn't become vegetarians for a few more years, so our food was not much different from everyone else at the time, with one big exception. We belonged to a gourmet dinner group and food expectations were high. Neither Joe nor I are sure how we got to be included in this group. None of the members were friends in any other context. One husband and wife were Swiss and he was a professional chef. Although Bettina, my friend from St. Louis Park, was not in the group, I think she was a friend with the couple from Switzerland. Maybe she suggested us, since she knew I liked to cook. I have some vague recollection that is what happened. Anyway, we were happy to be included. We rotated houses every other month and the host did most of the dinner with the exception of a few side dishes and dessert. The host would pick the theme or tell the other members the entrée so that they could make dishes compatible. The food was always outstanding and the evenings pleasant. We never became close friends with anyone from this group and did not see one another outside of our dinner parties. What we had in common was an interest in cooking, entertaining and being with pleasant people. It worked for two years. The chef and his family moved, we would be moving shortly and everyone felt it had run its course. The following is a menu of the food I prepared for one of the dinners at our home:

**Quiche Aux Fruits de Mer**
Scallops, crab, shallots, white wine, heavy cream, eggs, tomato paste in a pastry shell. Swiss cheese on top. (an enhanced repeat of the quiches I made for the baby shower in Roxbury)


**Soupe a l'oignon**
The classic with garlic croutons and lots of cheese.


**Artichouts au Naturel**
(I must have had that baby shower on my mind…I finally got to serve artichokes.) Served with a vinaigrette


**Veau**
Veal breast stuffed with sausage, ham, truffles, and breadcrumbs; seasoned with thyme, cloves, nutmeg and pepper.

I actually remember finding a wonderful store in Minneapolis that sold truffles and they helped me select the veal. I must have spent a fortune.


I never noted the other contributions. I am sure they were complex, as each of us was competing for the spotlight.

One adult night and, for me, memorable, was New Year's Eve. We had a baby sitter, a nursing student who was not on call and had no plans. Having Joe off and a sitter would have made it memorable even if we did nothing more than walk around the block. But we had big plans. Five other couples, all good friends, were also free. We drove to a nearby ski mountain. Now skiing in Minneapolis is not New England or Utah. It is cold enough for real snow but the mountain was an overgrown hill. It was a short drive away and a clear starry night. As we were skiing, gentle snowflakes started to fall. It was a magical setting. It was so unreal that you could easily imagine Disney characters singing while they skied down the slopes.

By 10, we were giddy with the true exhilaration of skiing and the pure beauty of the night but it was starting to get cold and we were all hungry. We piled into our cars and were back at our home a little after 10. With the babysitter taken home, we were ready to greet the New Year properly. We had Champagne and caviar to start. By 1, it was time to serve an apple pie that I had made earlier in the day. It was in a 10'' pie plate and the pie was at least 10" high. With the help of my two young children, it had been seasoned with an excess of cinnamon, ginger, cloves and nutmeg and sugar. The crust: Julia's recipe, lots of butter. Without a doubt it was the best pie I have ever made and I make a lot of pies. I have never been able to make one that tasted just like that New Year's Eve pie. Maybe you have to eat apple pie after a romantic evening ski. Maybe you have to be listening to wonderful tales: like the one Dennis told us that night. He grew up on a chicken farm. The rest of us were city or suburban kids and his farm tales with his rich Arkansas accent definitely went well with the spicy pie. We all rolled into bed hours later than any of us had done in years, but were feeling well enough the next morning to meet with our children at the zoo. The toddlers didn't care that the temperature was close to zero. There were enormous turtles walking around and that was, for them, as wondrous as skiing on New Year's Eve.

# APPLE PIE

I often increase any pie recipe so it will fill a 10" pie plate. I love the way a pie looks when it is large and high. This recipe is for a 9" pan since that is the most common size. It you want a more dramatic look, increase the recipe by half or more.

This pie is not my "famous" apple pie because I never wrote down what I did. It is a close approximation to the spices I used. You will have to determine the amounts to your taste.

CRUST:
I always use the recipe in Julia Child's *Mastering the Art of French Cooking* . Any good piecrust recipe that is made mostly with butter and a small amount of liquid oil works well. The butter is for the flavor and the oil is for flakiness. I have tried recipes with sour cream instead of the water and that creates an interesting texture and taste.

| | |
|---|---|
| Apples | 6 to 8 large tart, peeled and sliced |
| Sugar | 1 cup plus 1/4 cup (more or less to taste ) |
| Flour | 1/2 cup |
| Butter | 1/4 stick, melted |
| Cinnamon | 2 tsp. |
| Nutmeg | 1/2 tsp. |
| Cloves | 1/8 tsp., ground |
| Allspice | ¼ tsp. |
| Mace | 1/8 tsp. |
| Lemon peel | ½ tsp. |

PROCEDURE:

1. Toss the apples with 1 cup of sugar, spices and lemon peel.
   \*\*you may want to mix the sugar and spices together first and then dip and apple piece into the mixture to see if you like it.
2. Fill the pastry-lined pie plate with the seasoned apples.
   \*\*Make sure you prick the crust with a fork, creating many small holes over the bottom.
3. Combine 1/4 cup flour and a 1/4 cup sugar. Sprinkle over the top of spiced apples.
4. Drizzle the melted butter on top of flour and sugar.
5. Cover the apples with a pastry crust, cutting three air holes.
6. I used leftover pie dough to make leaves that get "glued" to the crust with an egg wash. Use the egg wash (an egg beaten with a tsp. of water) to cover the top crust.
7. Bake 350 until golden brown and juices bubble out a bit.

Summer 1969 (the day we left for our trip)

It was while living in our house in Dinkytown (the neighborhood surrounding the University) that we started to explore and took our first family vacation. We went to the Badlands of South Dakota in a big old Chevy Greenbrier (looked like a VW bus). We bought it used and it was old and battered but perfect for our planned tent camping trip. Wendy was five months and Jon was two years old (what were we thinking?) If you have ever driven through South Dakota, I am sure what I am about to tell you will be familiar. Along the highway, every few miles you would see a large sign: "Wall Drug"… and then telling you how many more miles. These signs went on for close to 100 miles. Joe and I agreed that we were not stopping at Wall Drug. It had to be awful. The signs were annoying and we had already picked our lunch stopping point. The car had a different plan. Just as we are approaching Wall Drug, the car died. The car was dead, but the town had one gas station (thank goodness), the famous drug store (which is a mega tourist spot), and that is all I remember seeing. The gas station guy said he was going to the dump to see if he could find some used parts to get our car going, but in the meantime we should enjoy a lunch at the drugstore. And so we spent the next four hours at Wall Drug and all I can say is "thank goodness it was there." It was large, clean and they were happy to let the four of us hang out. Back on the road, we were off to the Black Hills. It was late summer and we set up camp in a spot that was too beautiful to be real, until it started to snow. We were in a tent and cold. Tomorrow would surely be a better day.

We woke at dawn to more snow! So much for summer camping in the Black Hills. The rest of our trip we spent in a lovely cabin. This was the beginning of our love as a family of the mountains, skiing in the winter and hiking in the summer. We did do tent camping many times after this misadventure and they always were fun when it didn't rain or wasn't buggy or noisy. After a few years we declared no more tents and bought a cabin of our own.

Okay, I agree. Joe does not look very happy and has that Albert Einstein hairdo, but this was definitely our camping, hiking look.

What philosopher said that all good things must come to an end? Our time in that wonderful big house in an ideal location was about to come to an end.

One afternoon while the children were napping, my doorbell rang. The young woman ringing my bell and knocking on the door was our landlord's wife. I invited her in, made her tea and we sat in the living room: she on the blue couch and me in the old rocking chair that was a treasure from our days in Boston. We didn't know one another, but she lived in the neighborhood so I thought this was a social call. Once the tea was gone and some sweet bread eaten, she left. Early that evening while I was making dinner and the children were whining for attention the phone rang. It was the landlord. Without any niceties, he told me his wife loved the house we were living in and wanted to move there. We had until the end of the month to move out. That was that.

Who knew to get a lease? So we needed to find a new place to live, pack up our belongings, spread throughout our two-story house plus a basement and a yard with play equipment, and smile all the while. I was furious. Joe was furious but way too busy being a medical resident to know what else we could do.

This is what I might have served with tea. I made these breads in small loaf pans, put them in the freezer and gave them to neighbors and friends or served to visitors.

## APRICOT BREAD

| | |
|---|---|
| Apricots | ½ lb. dried |
| Walnuts | 3 Tbsp. chopped |
| Butter | ¾ cups |
| Flour | 2 ½ cups |
| Sugar | ¾ cup |
| Baking powder | ½ tsp. |
| Salt | ½ tsp. |
| Baking soda | 1 tsp. |
| Butter | 1 cup |
| Egg | 1 |

1. Coarsely chop apricots and cook in 1 cup of water.
2. Simmer for 10 minutes or until most of the water is absorbed.
3. Drain the apricots and reserve the liquid in a 1 cup measuring cup.
4. Coarsely chop walnuts.
5. Melt the butter and set aside.
6. Mix together the flour, sugar, baking powder, salt and soda.
7. Add the chopped nuts.
8. Add to the apricot juice enough buttermilk to measure 1 cup.
9. Make a well in the dry ingredients and add the liquid and the beaten egg.
10. Add the apricots.
11. Put in prepared loaf pan.
12. Bake 350 degrees for about 1 hour and 15 minutes.

## ALMOND BREAD

| | |
|---|---|
| Almonds | ½ lb. |
| Flour | 1/2 cup |
| Baking powder | 1/2 tsp. |
| Salt | 1/8 tsp. |
| Butter | 1/2 cup |
| Vanilla extract | 2 tsp. |
| Almond extract | 1/4 tsp. |
| Sugar | 1/2 cup plus 2 Tbsp. |
| Eggs | 2, beaten |

1. Almonds: fine grind 1 cup, chop the remaining.
2. Mix together the flour, powder and salt.
3. Cream together the butter and the two extracts.
4. Add the sugar and beat until fluffy.
5. Add the eggs slowly until well blended.
6. Put the batter in a loaf pan.
7. Bake 350 degrees for 1 hour.

## Northeast Minneapolis

Spring in Northeast Minneapolis (window open and snow on the ground)

Our eviction brought us to northeast Minneapolis. This was a family centered neighborhood: ranch-style houses with big backyards, BBQ's, garages, three bedrooms and wall papered eat-in kitchens. We had a screened porch that extended our eating space during short, hot Minneapolis summers. Wendy's bedroom backed up to the porch, so we had to limit our use to when she was awake. I do remember having a big dinner party and using the porch. It was my first attempt at ratatouille. I served it with a cheese soufflé. It was an elegant light supper. The dessert was a strawberry Charlotte made with whipped cream, butter, strawberries and ladyfingers. All three of these recipes…Julia's. I remember spending hours cutting the vegetables so they were all the same size and shape and cooking each to the right tenderness. Now I just take the eggplant, zucchini, peppers, onions and tomatoes, cut them in chunks and throw them in a pot.

Living in this house with two children and a dog, we knew we were again a stereotype. We were that family: you know, a boy, a girl, a dog, a ranch house and two cars in the garage. I thought I would hate it, but I didn't. My neighbors were friendly and they taught us to BBQ. Even the dog, an attempt to be unique, only made us more like everyone else. We got a Norwegian Elkhound, a dog neither of us had ever seen. Maybe not in Boston, but in Minnesota they were the dog of choice. There were even Elkhound picnic days. Everyone with Scandinavian ancestry would go and when we called "Elky" to come to us, every female dog at the park came running.

Our son was at preschool at the University of Minnesota lab school. Most of my friends were at home with young children. I didn't know anyone who was working. Sure, we tried to appear to be more than "housewives," but even with the League of Women Voters, book clubs, or volunteering, we knew we were housewives like in any silly 1950's sitcom. No, we didn't wear dresses and high heels when doing housework, but the internal message was the same. Jeans and sweatshirts did not change the feelings that we could do more. One day while waiting for my son to get out of class I met a mother I had never seen before. We had an interesting conversation. She told me that it was her day off and that she taught at the University full time. She saw the surprise on my face, and then, I have never forgotten what she said.

"We give our son quality time not quantity time."

It took a few years, but by the time Wendy was in preschool, I was a working mom. But not yet! Not in Minneapolis. So I cooked, and tried to be the best mother and wife, just like June Cleaver and all the rest of the 1960s brides.

The only kitchen photo I could find

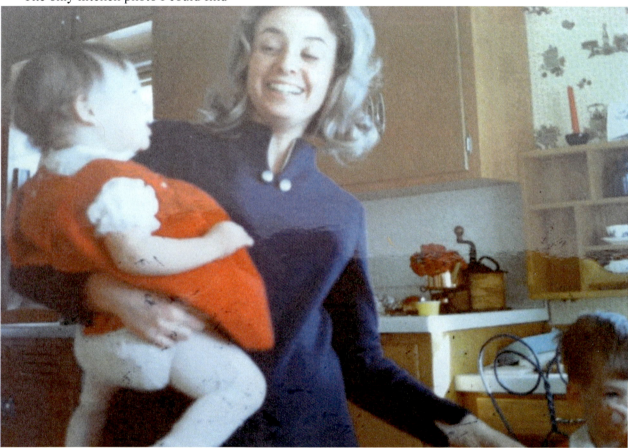

A few more 1960's recipes:

## TOURNADOS ROSSINI

One very special evening, Joe and I were taken to an elegant restaurant in Minneapolis. We normally never got to eat in anything but the local spaghetti restaurant in Dinkytown. As an aside, it was at this Italian restaurant that I learned that adding fennel seeds to pasta sauce is wonderful. But, back to the elegant night out. We ordered Tornados Rossini, having seen it in many cookbooks but I had not made it. Tournados Rossini was now on my "to do" list. It turns out to be easy to make if you cut a few corners (canned artichoke bottoms and store bought pâté). This is a very expensive dish and only for special occasions.

(for 4 people)

| | |
|---|---|
| Artichoke bottoms | 4 large ones. You can cook 4 artichokes, eat the leaves and save the bottoms or buy them in a can. |
| Pâté de Foie Gras | 4 slices, at least 1/4 " thick |
| Madeira | 6 Tbsp. |
| Beef stock | 3/4 cup |
| Butter | 5 Tbsp. |
| Truffles | 12 slices (this is not mandatory but does add to the panache) |
| Steak filets | 4, at least 1 inch thick |
| Bacon | 4 pieces |
| Cooking string | |

PROCEDURE:

1. Slice artichoke bottoms so they are thin enough to be flat. Season with salt and pepper.
2. Place the pâté slices in a dish and marinate in 2 Tbsp. Madeira and 2 Tbsp. beef stock.
3. Place the truffles in a small saucepan with 2 Tbsp. Madeira and 1Tbsp. butter. Warm.
4. Cook the steaks:
    a. Wrap each steak with bacon and tie with string to hold the bacon around the circumference.
    b. Sauté in butter in heavy skillet for 8 to 10 minutes to medium rare.
5. Arrange the warmed artichoke bottoms on each plate. Place the steak on top to the artichokes. On top of the steak, place the pâté and a few slices of truffles.

Sauce:
Put remaining beef broth in the skillet that you cooked the beef.
Boil down until reduces by half. Mix 2Tbsp. cornstarch with 2Tbsp. Madeira with 3Tbsp. butter. Add to the broth and simmer for about a minute. Pour sauce on top.

# SPINACH ROLL

This spinach roll found itself on many buffet tables. It is a nice color, texture and taste and it can be made in advance.

| | |
|---|---|
| Butter | 6 Tbsp. |
| Flour | 1/2 cup |
| Milk | 2 cups |
| Eggs | 5 (separate) |
| Shallots | 4 chopped |
| Mushrooms | 6 medium diced |
| Spinach | 1 cup, cooked and chopped |
| Mustard | 1 Tbsp. |
| Nutmeg | 1/4 tsp. |
| Cream cheese | 6 oz., softened. |
| Salt | |
| Pepper | |

PROCEDURE:

Preheat oven to 400 degrees
1. Grease and line with wax paper (current update: parchment paper) 15 1/2 by 10 1/2 jellyroll pan.
2. Melt 4 Tbsp. butter in a saucepan. Blend in the flour and 1/2 tsp. of salt and 1/2 tsp. pepper. Gradually stir in the milk. Cook for 1 minute until you have a sauce.
3. Beat 5 egg yolks to blend. Add a small amount at a time of the milk and flour sauce while beating until it is well blended. Cool to room temperature.
4. Beat the 5 egg whites until stiff but not dry. Fold into cool sauce.
5. Spread in prepared pan.
6. Bake 25 to 30 minutes until well puffed and browned. Turn immediately onto a clean towel. Spread with warm filling (recipe to follow) and roll with aid of the towel sliding it to a serving platter that is oven proof. The roll can be kept warm in a low oven or reheated if necessary.
7. Use a serrated knife to slice and serve with Parmesan cheese.

Filling procedure:
1. Spinach. Make sure the cooked and chopped spinach is dry.
2. Melt 2 Tbsp. of butter in a skillet. Sauté shallots.
3. Add the mushrooms and cook until moisture is evaporated.
4. Add the spinach, nutmeg and cream cheese and heat until the ingredients are combined. Season with salt and pepper.

# GREEK STYLE MEATBALLS

Always a fan of lemon and mint, these simple meatballs were my favorite. I made them golf ball size for dinner with rice or smaller for a hot appetizer as part of a buffet.

| | |
|---|---|
| Ground beef | 1lb. |
| Rice | 1/3 cup, long grain, uncooked |
| Garlic | 1 clove, minced |
| Onion | 1 finely chopped |
| Parsley | 2 Tbsp., finely chopped |
| Mint | 1-2 tsp., dried or 1/2 cup fresh |
| Egg | 4 |
| Bread crumbs | 1/2 cup, finely ground |
| Chicken broth | 1 to 1 1/2 cups |
| Lemon | Juice from 2 or 3 large lemons |

PROCEDURE:

1. Combine beef, rice, onion, garlic, parsley, mint, salt and pepper, and breadcrumbs. Add 2 eggs and mix well.
2. Make meatballs about the size of a ping-pong ball (walnut size if using in a buffet).
3. Heat the broth in a large pot. Add the meatballs and simmer for about 45 minutes.
4. Whisk together 2 eggs and the lemon juice. Add one cup of the hot broth to the egg and lemon juice mixture. Add slowly so the egg does not curdle. 5.Remove the pot from the heat and add the lemon/egg mixture. Reheat slowly.

# EGGPLANT PARMESAN

I think of eggplant as universal. You can use it with any seasonings and cooking style. I expect that I will include many eggplant dishes through the decades. It has been one of the few constants. Sorry my children do not love it as much as I do.

| | |
|---|---|
| Eggplant | 1 large globe eggplant, peeled |
| Breadcrumbs | 1 1/2 cup (approx.) |
| Oregano | |
| Basil | 2 tsp. for each |
| Parsley | |
| Salt and pepper | |
| Egg | 2 beaten |
| Onion | 1 diced |
| Carrot | 1 diced |
| Olive oil | |
| Fennel seeds | 1/4 tsp., crushed |
| Garlic | 1 clove, minced |
| Tomatoes | 1 large can plum tomatoes |
| Red wine | 1/4 cup (optional) |

PROCEDURE:

1. Sauté the onion and carrot in olive oil. Add the fennel seeds and garlic.
2. Add the red wine and cook until the vegetables are soft and the wine is cooked down.
3. Add the tomatoes, 1 tsp. basil, 1 tsp. oregano, 1 tsp. parsley and cook for 15 minutes.
4. Puree the mixture in a blender (food processor today).
   The carrot adds sweetness to the sauce and is best if pureed. Another option is to puree the carrots and onion prior to adding the tomatoes.
5. Mix 1 tsp. each of the oregano, parsley and basil in the breadcrumbs.   Salt and pepper to taste.
6. Slice the eggplant into 1/2" slices. Dip each slice in the egg batter and then in the seasoned breadcrumbs.
7. Brown the eggplant on both sides in a fry pan with olive oil.
8. Put sauce on the bottom of a baking dish. Place the eggplant slices on top of the sauce and then cover the slices with the rest of the sauce.
9. Mozzarella cheese on top of each eggplant slice.

Bake 350 degrees until eggplant is soft and sauce bubbling.

*Alternatives:*
1. Use a smaller baking dish and stack the eggplant with alternate layers of cheese. Three layers of eggplant are ideal.
2. Layer the eggplant with cheese and tofu: layer 1 eggplant, then cheese, then eggplant and then tofu and then eggplant and topped with cheese.

# RUGELACH

This is a favorite pastry of Russian Jewish immigrants and is now seen in almost every bakery and even in some supermarkets. This is a simple recipe but I think the best. It came to me from a friend of my mother in laws. I wish I remembered her name.

| | |
|---|---|
| Cream Cheese | 1 cup |
| Butter | 1/2 lb. |
| Flour | 2 cups |
| Cinnamon | |
| Walnuts, chopped | |
| Sugar | |

This recipe has been handed down from three generations and no one ever measured the sugar, cinnamon and nuts. It is all done to taste. Take a cup of sugar, add enough cinnamon to taste and color. You might need more or less. Once you make this recipe the first time, you can better judge how much you use for your second attempt. Trust me, you will make them again. Finely chop a lot of nuts and, if you have too much, make a coffee cake another day.

PROCEDURE:

1. Mix the sour cream, butter and flour together.
2. Wrap the dough and chill for two hours (or longer if you want).
3. Divide the dough into 3 equal parts.
4. Roll each batch of dough into a circle about 8" or 9" round.
5. Sprinkle each circle with the sugar and cinnamon mixture.
6. Sprinkle the circles with the finely chopped nuts.
7. Cut each circle into 16 wedges (like cutting a pie).
8. Roll each wedge starting from the wide end first.
9. Place all the rugelach on ungreased cookie sheets. You can use parchment paper but it is not necessary.

Bake for 25 minutes in a preheated 350 oven. These are great hot, room temperature or right out of the freezer, still frozen.

No landscaping but a great house. That is Jonathan at the front door

### LEAVENWORTH KANSAS   1971-1973

With the success of the ranch house experience in Minneapolis, we had the opportunity to do it again. This time the move was a demand from "Uncle Sam." It was the height of the Vietnam War, and all physicians were expected to serve in some capacity. The options were few but Joe took his chances and applied to the Public Health Service. He was accepted. Now the next step was where he was going to be sent. The Public Health Service at the time was part of the Navy. Doctors had three major choices, or at least these were the only ones Joe considered. You could be a doctor at an Indian Reservation, a doctor at a Federal Prison or work in Washington. Joe's choice was an Indian reservation but felt any of the three would be better than going to Vietnam and be in a war we disapproved of. I was home when the bureau called to tell us of his assignment. No, not an Indian Reservation, and not his last choice Washington, but Leavenworth Kansas at a Federal Prison. I cried a bit, then got my composure and called Joe. We were so set to go to an Indian Reservation we had to quickly change our mind set. We had two young children and we were going to a prison! Now, this was not just any prison. This was "The Prison."

Our next home for the next two years was a three-bedroom ranch with a large backyard. The difference between this ranch and Minneapolis was that it had bigger bedrooms, a walkout basement family room (great for hanging out during tornadoes), a nice big kitchen and views of the federal prison. This also meant that most of our neighbors worked at the "big house" or were connected to the army war college, Ft. Leavenworth. Ft. Leavenworth is the military base famous for its "War College" that attracted high-level military officers. The base was upscale with swimming pools, restaurants and shopping. Even the on-base housing was nice, but not as great as our new home.

My memories of our two years in Leavenworth have a lot to do with the kitchen. We did a lot of entertaining and lots of cooking. We had more time together as a family than ever before since Joe had to keep strict regulation hours (8 a.m. to 4 p.m.), unless there was a medical emergency.

Some of my best cooking came out of that kitchen. This was the time when I was wrapping lots of things in pastry: Beef Wellington, pâté en croute, and stuffed chicken breasts. One en croute dish had the potential to be lethal; only pure luck saved my guests. It was Joe's birthday. Our dinner was to start with pâté en croute. I pureed the livers in my blender. There was too much in the blender and nothing was happening, so I took a wooden spoon and pushed the mixture as it was blending. All looked smooth and I continued with the recipe. Later that day, I noticed that a small piece of my wooden spoon was missing. I shrugged my shoulders and went on doing whatever else was occupying my attention. The evening of the party, one of our guests found the piece—whole, not in a million slivers—as he bit into his pate. Horrified, I told everyone to stop eating. No one did. They just combed through their slices, and once assured there was no wood, they continued to eat.

Memories of that evening are of young adults dressed not quite 'hippie" but also not very sophisticated, and clearly trying to look dressed up. We ate pâté en croute while sitting on a "couch." This couch was really Wendy's old crib. We had painted it yellow and covered the mattress with a yellow and green print fabric. The hanging light fixture was an upside down terracotta flowerpot. I wish I could find a photo. It was one of our more creative endeavors.

The pâté en croute and my "hippie trying to be stylish" dress…hmmm.
Curtains came with the house and do not go with my red, white and blue dishes that I had recently purchased at the PX at Fort Leavenworth.

# PÂTE

My first attempt at Pâté was in Minneapolis, but the "En Croute" started in Kansas

| | |
|---|---|
| Chicken livers | 1 lb. |
| Onion | 1/2 cup, chopped |
| Butter | 1/4 cup |
| Egg yolks | 2 |
| Cream | 1/4 cup |
| Flour | 1 Tbsp. |
| Cognac | 2 Tbsp. |
| Salt, pepper | |
| Tarragon to taste | |

PROCEDURE:

1. Cook onions and livers in butter.
2. Add the yolks and mix with the cream.
3. Add all the other ingredients.
4. Puree in blender until smooth.
5. Pour into a buttered loaf pan. Cover with buttered parchment paper.
6. Put loaf pan in a pan of hot water with the water coming halfway up the sides of the loaf pan.
7. Bake 300 degrees for 1 hour.
8. Serve with French bread. OR
1. Make a puff pastry dough or rich pastry dough.
2. Grease the back of a loaf pan and cover with parchment paper.
3. Take 1/2 of the dough and drape it over the back of the loaf pan.
4. Prick the dough with a fork so it does not puff up.
5. Bake the pastry shell in 350 degrees for about 25 minutes.
6. Cool the shell and remove very carefully from the pan.
7. Fill the shell with the pâté mixture.
8. Roll out the remaining dough and cover the top, pressing the sides to the bottom crust.
9. If you have extra pastry, decorate the top with cutout shapes such as leaves.
10. Cover the top with an egg wash (beaten egg and milk).
11. Bake 350 degrees for about 45 minutes. If crust is getting too brown, make a tent cover with foil.
12. Serve at room temperature.

# BEEF WELLINGTON

Beef Wellington is what I made for company in the 70s and although it is Julia Child's recipe, this decade would not be represented without including the recipe. When we moved to Kansas we had full use of the PX. Buying a top quality fillet of beef was inexpensive. What should have stretched our budget made barely a dent. The time and effort were worth it. By the time we moved to Marblehead, Massachusetts I had perfected this grand dish and even though the beef now cost more than four times what we had been spending, I continued to need to wow our guests. By the end of the 70s, we no longer ate beef but I had already made my mark on our guests, so I stopped making Beef Wellington. My son, born in 1967, could not have been more than 10 by the time I stopped serving fillet of beef in pastry but he remembers it well and still reminds me of the company Beef Wellington.

Giving full credit to Julia Child, here is her recipe:

## FILET OF BEEF WELLINGTON
(Whole Tenderloin of Beef Baked in Pastry)

For 8 people

Take tenderloin of beef, marinate it in herbs and wine, cover it with a rich cloak of mushrooms, bake it in decorated pastry, and you have Filet of Beef Wellington. This is a splendid dish when you want to make a vast impression on your guests, and if you have prepared all the various elements a day ahead of time, the assembling and cooking are easy indeed. Have the outside membrane and all excess fat removed from the tenderloin, but have the suet (fat covering) saved. Have the tail or small end turned back over the meat to make an even cylinder about 12 inches long, and have the meat tied at 1-" intervals around the circumference.

Optional Marinade

Although the tenderloin is the most expensive part of the beef, it has the least flavor. A 24-hour marinade will give it more character, and you can use the marinade again, for making the sauce. 1/3 cup light olive oil or cooking oil   A small heavy saucepan   1/2 cup each of sliced onions, carrots, and celery stalks   1/4 tsp. each of dried thyme and sage   1 bay leaf   3 allspice berries or cloves   6 peppercorns   An oval casserole or baking dish 12 inches long   1 tsp. salt   1 cup dry white vermouth   1/3 cup cognac   Place the oil in the saucepan and add the vegetables are herbs; cover the pan and cook slowly until vegetables are tender--about 10 minutes. Place the tenderloin in casserole or baking dish, sprinkle with salt, cover with the cooked vegetable mixture, and pour on the wine and cognac. Cover and refrigerate. Turn and baste the meat every several hours for at least 24 hours. Just before the next step, scrape off marinade and dry meat in paper towels.

Preliminary Baking

Before it is cooked in pastry, the tenderloin has a preliminary baking to stiffen it, so it will hold its shape in the crust.   1 Tb cooking oil,  shallow roasting pan

(Preheat oven to 425 degrees F.)    Rub the meat with the oil and place in roasting pan. If you have saved the suet, place it over the beef to protect and baste it during roasting. (Lacking suet, you will have to baste the meat with oil every 5 minutes during roasting.) Set in upper third of oven and roast for 25 minutes, turning and basting the meat once with the fat in the pan. Remove from oven and let cool for 30 minutes or longer. If you are doing this ahead of time, wrap and refrigerate the meat when it is cold; bring to room temperature before final cooking.

The Mushroom Flavoring

   This is a mushroom duxelles with wine and foie gras, which bakes around the meat.   2 lbs. mushrooms   2 Tb butter   4 Tb minced shallots or scallions   1/2 cup dry Sercial Madeira   Salt and pepper   4 to 5 mousses de foie or foie gras   Trim, wash, and dry mushrooms; chop them into small pieces less than 1/8 " in size. You will have about 6 cups of minced mushrooms; so that they will cook dry, which is necessary for this recipe, twist them, a handful at a time, in the corner of a towel to extract as much juice as possible. Save juice for the sauce. Then sauté the mushrooms for 7 to 8 minutes in the butter with the shallots or scallions; when mushroom pieces begin to separate from each other, add the Madeira and boil rapidly until liquid has evaporated. Season to taste with salt and pepper, and beat in the mousse de foie or foie gras. Refrigerate in a covered bowl; beat to soften just before using.

The Pastry

   The beef is baked and served en croute or in a piecrust dough. Use the following proportions:   3 cups all-purpose flour (scoop cup into bag, level off with straight-edged knife)   1 3/4 sticks (7 oz.) chilled butter   4 Tb chilled shortening   2 tsp. salt   3/4 cup iced water   Blend together all the ingredients listed and chill for 2 hours before using. So that the crust will be crisp when served, it is done in two parts: a cooked bottom case to hold the beef, and a flaky dough topping.

The Bottom Pastry Case

Butter the outside of a loaf-shaped tin approximately 12 by 3 1/4 inches bottom diameter, and 3 inches deep. Roll about three fifths of the chilled pastry into a rectangle 16 by 7 inches, and 1/8 inch thick. Lay pastry on upside-down tin, press in place, and trim so pastry forms a case 1 1/2 inches deep. With the tines of a table fork, prick sides and bottom of dough at 1/4-inch intervals to keep it from puffing in the oven, and chill at least half an hour to relax the dough. Bake until very lightly browned in middle of a preheated 425-degree oven for 12 to 15 minutes. Let cool 10 minutes on tin, then unmold. (Case may be refrigerated or frozen.)

The Pastry Topping

Roll remaining dough into a 16X7-inch rectangle, spread bottom half with 1 1/2 Tbsp.'s cold but soft butter and fold in half to enclose butter. Repeat with another 1 1/2 Tbsp. butter. Roll again into a rectangle and fold in thirds, as though folding a business letter. This is now mock puff pastry, with layers of butter between layers of dough; it will be light and flaky when baked. Chill for 2 hours, then roll into a 16X10-inch rectangle. Cut a 3-inch strip from the long end and reserve for decorations; lay large rectangle flat on a baking sheet lined with waxed paper; cover with waxed paper and a damp towel, and refrigerate.

The Decorations   Cut strips, circles, diamonds, or leaf shapes from the 3-inch strip and chill with the pastry topping.

Assembling and Baking the Beef Wellington

The beef takes about 45 minutes to bake, and should rest for 20 minutes before carving and serving. It is assembled just before baking.

Assembling
   Place the baked pastry case on a baking and serving platter or a buttered baking sheet and spread half of the mushroom mixture in the bottom of the case. Remove trussing strings and set the beef in the case, covering the meat with the remaining mushrooms. Paint sides of case with egg glaze (1 egg beaten with 1/2 tsp. water), lay pastry topping over meat allowing the edges to fall down about 1 " on sides of case; press pastry onto sides of case. Paint pastry topping with glaze, affix decorations, and paint again with glaze. Make crosshatch marking over glaze with a knife, to give texture to the glaze when baked. Make three 1/8-inch vent holes centered about 3 inches apart in top of pastry and insert paper or foil funnels for escaping steam. Plunge a meat thermometer through central hole and into center of meat.

Bake for 20 to 25 minutes in middle level of a preheated 425-degree oven or until pastry has started to brown. Then lower thermostat to 375 degrees and bake 20 to 25 minutes more, or to a meat thermometer reading of 137 degrees for rare beef. Let rest at a temperature of not more than 120 degrees for at least 20 minutes before serving, so juices will retreat back into meat tissues before carving. (To serve, carve as though cutting a sausage into 1 1/2-inch slices. Pastry will crumble slightly as you carve the beef; a very sharp serrated knife will minimize this.)

Sauce Simmer marinade ingredients and mushroom juices with 2 cups beef bouillon and 1 tablespoon tomato paste for 1 hour; when reduced to 2 cups, strain, degrease, season, and thicken with 2 Tbsp. of cornstarch beaten with 1/4 cup of Madeira.  Sauce Perigueux. Simmer 1 or 2 minced canned truffles and their juice for a moment in the sauce madere.   Sauce Colbert. Just before serving, 1 cup of sauce béarnaise gradually into 2 cups of sauce Madera.

*The French Chef Cookbook*, Julia Child [Alfred A. Knopf:New York] 1972 (p. 296-300)

After Kansas we would never eat or live like that again. It wasn't that I would lose my interest in cooking, quite the opposite. It was because towards the end of our time in Kansas we were becoming aware of new beliefs about nutrition and were gradually moving away from rich food. It would be another few years before we became vegetarians. It would only be one more year before the crib and the upside down flowerpot would go to the dump and we would lose our carefree sense of home decor and move to real furniture and sensible food. But that comes later. We still have many more Kansas adventures.

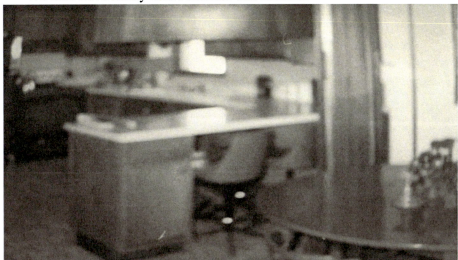
Leavenworth Kitchen

This fuzzy photo is all I could find but it does bring back a mouse memory. For over a week, a mouse would greet me every morning, always sitting on top of the stove. He would scamper away after we nodded good morning. He avoided all traps set with peanut butter and cheese and was only seen in the morning. The morning he didn't show up, I felt a small sadness. I missed our early morning date. This was a contrast to my Minneapolis experience when I ran from our apartment leaving a mouse and my sleeping son behind.

Joe's rendition of my kitchen mouse.

# SALMON COULIBIAC

A classic recipe found in many fine cookbooks during this period of time and it fit my interest in wrapping stuff in pastry. For this recipe I used the packaged frozen puff pastry that you can find in most markets. I could have made my own puff pastry as it is not complicated (just lots of butter and time) but for this recipe I find the frozen variety an excellent way to save some time and still have the "wow" factor.

| | |
|---|---|
| Frozen pastry dough | 2 sheets |
| Eggs | 3, two hard boiled 1 beaten in a small bowl |
| Spinach | 3 cup steamed and dried |
| Mushrooms | 1/2 lb. sliced |
| Onion | 1 sliced and lightly sauté (do not brown) |
| Salmon | 3 to 4lbs. |
| Thyme | 1tsp. |
| Dill | 1tsp. |
| Salt and pepper | |

PROCEDURE:
1. Defrost the 2 sheets of pastry dough. Brush one sheet with beaten egg mixed with 1 Tbsp. of water.
2. Place the cooked and dried spinach on top of the pastry.
3. Place the sliced mushrooms on top of the spinach.
4. Place the salmon on top of the mushrooms and spinach.
5. Season the salmon with salt, pepper, thyme and dill.
6. Chop the two hard boiled eggs and spread on top of the salmon.
7. The next layer: place the sliced onions.
8. The final layer: the 2nd sheet of pastry. Press the sides of the bottom layer of pastry with the top layer.
9. Brush the pastry with the egg wash.
10. Cover a baking sheet with parchment paper and move the salmon to the prepared baking sheet.
11. Bake 350 degrees for 45 minutes.
12. Let the salmon rest in turned off oven for 20 minutes until slicing.
    1. Beat in 1/8 tsp. white pepper, 1/4 tsp. cayenne pepper and 2 1/2 tsp. salt and the dill. (The level of seasoning can be checked by dropping a tsp. of the mixture into simmering water for two minutes. Do not taste uncooked)
    2. Butter a 9x5x3 loaf pan.
    3. Spoon 1/2 half of the sole mixture into the pan. Arrange the salmon pieces lengthwise over the fish mixture, leaving a space between the two pieces.
    4. Spoon the remaining fillet mixture over the salmon and spread evenly.
    5. Cover with buttered parchment paper and set in a roasting pan with boiling water extended up the sides of the pan about half way.
    6. Bake for 45 minutes or until loaf feels set when lightly touched.
    7. Chill for several hours or overnight.
    8. Turn onto a serving platter and garnish with cucumber, lemon slices and dill.
    9. I have also served this with a yogurt, dill and cucumber mixture as a sauce.

Plant based diets during our time in Kansas were not necessarily about being a vegetarian. In the 1970s in Kansas, it was marijuana. It grew wild everywhere. Being a bit older than some of our friends, we had come to this point in our lives without ever trying it or knowing anyone who admitted to using marijuana. Not telling us, one of our closest friends made brownies that I thought were very dry and not sweet enough. I couldn't figure out why I got the giggles and wanted more brownies. Before I took my second, I was told the truth and could now add marijuana brownies to my growing recipe file, although I never did make them. It just didn't seem right with two young kids around who loved brownies.

It wasn't just our friends who had an interest in this plant. The horses that we rode loved to take nibbles as they trotted through the fields. One day, the field would be filled with marijuana plants and the next week the entire field would have been burned. (The government trying to control the growth would do these regular burns. Can you imagine the air?) I think when nutritionists talk about a "plant based" diet this is not what they have in mind.

Jon and Wendy dressing up

While we lived in Leavenworth, Jonathan started kindergarten and Wendy went to a morning preschool in a neighbor's basement. It was actually very good: nurturing and stimulating. I found an interesting job one day a week. I have told you about the federal prison and the army base but what I didn't tell you was that there were three other prisons: a men's state prison, a women's state prison and the county jail. I worked at the women's prison in a 1:1 "friendship" program. I was assigned a female prisoner and I was to be her link to the outside world. Oh boy, what a learning experience that was. I was not yet 30 years old and had lived a rather conventional middle class life. This woman and the others I got to know figured me out in two seconds. I was an easy mark. They knew I wanted them to like me and they milked it for all it was worth. I said "yes" to all the food they wanted me to bring them, I believed every story they told, and I fell for all their sweet-talking. "You are the nicest person I've ever met". "You have changed my life." It took me about six months to catch on and it was only when I got hit in the face with the truth.

One day, one of the women asked me how often I met with her parole officer. I told her I never did. I didn't meet with anyone, nor did I report to anyone. Everything they said to me didn't go anywhere. She was furious. All this buttering up was the con. She wanted me to pass the word along that she was reformed. I still continued to visit, but it was awful. She resented me no matter how hard I tried to redefine our relationship. I had one other "friend,' and that wasn't any better. I came to learn that the two women who had been assigned to me were lovers. They must have had a lot of laughs at my expense.

When we left Kansas and moved to Massachusetts, I started a master's degree program in counseling and family therapy. I wanted to learn how to do it right. Another lesson waiting to be learned, there is no "right," just a lot of educated guessing.

Leavenworth, a prison town, was also the town that I had three run-ins with the law. The first time was simple. A few friends were at the house with their preschoolers playing with Wendy. I looked at the clock and realized I was late to pick Jon up from morning kindergarten. I left my friends and Wendy while I dashed to the car and drove the three blocks. I got there in time to get my car in line with all the other mothers waiting for their children. A policeman was stopping at each car talking to every driver. I had no idea why. This was a legal pick up spot. It didn't take long to learn what he was up to and see his delight that he caught someone. I had run out of my house without my purse and did not have my license. My car plates were Minnesota (legal when you are military, as we were). But no driver's license was not legal. I explained that I lived three blocks away and would bring it right back to him. No way. "Ticket and a court date, lady. Now move on." A few weeks later I went to court, told my story, showed my license and was sent home with no fine or reprimand.

The next offense was on the army base. The rule on the army base was if any family member of an officer gets a ticket, it was the officer who got the reprimand. In other words, Joe was responsible for anything I did. The speed limit was 20 miles an hour. I was trying to drive slowly, but I guess not slowly enough. I was stopped, I cried, and I was dismissed with a warning. I was shaking all the way home. It really scared me.

The third time was a big deal and a complicated story. I will try to make it brief. Every week I took Jon to art classes in Kansas City. Wendy and I would explore the museum while he was creating great 5-year-old art. It was fun. The trip was mostly highway. The highway ended in Lansing, Kansas, which was the town abutting Leavenworth. It was a known speed trap. Everyone knew to drive slower than slow. I got off the highway, had kid friendly music on the radio and was staring at the road and my speedometer. It was just at this moment that something was going on between Jon and Wendy. Without turning around I made a hand motion for them to be quiet and told them that I had to concentrate. The next thing I knew, there were three state patrol cars pulling me over. "Please tell me what I did," I asked without trying to sound hysterical, as I had two impressionable passengers. "You know very well lady, we'll see you in court." And away they drove. It took every bit of will power to not cry and get these two inquiring children home and involved so I could call Joe.

After hours of people who knew people making calls, we learned that there was a patrol vehicle behind me bringing blood to a hospital. He had his lights on and was trying to pass me since I was going so SLOW. When I made the hand motion to the children, he thought I was telling him to bug off. I never even saw him. I needed a lawyer. We looked in the yellow pages, big mistake. We later learned we had hired the well-known town drunk. Nice, but not too sharp.

My lawyer thought I was in big trouble. The court date arrived. The kids were with a sitter, and I put on one of my "going to work" suits. Joe was in uniform. The trial was not in a courthouse, (there wasn't one), but in what looked like an office building. We walked in the front door and the room was filled with tall, very tall, patrol officers. They made a small aisle for Joe and me to walk through but they did not make it easy for us. Joe was not allowed in the room with me. I went in with my attorney, who was wearing an ill fitting, rumpled suit and sporting slicked back hair. The room was mostly one very large table. Seated around the table were state troopers and at the head was a small grey haired woman. I was told to sit to her left and my attorney next to me. She said she had read the trooper's account and now would like to hear my side of the story. "In your own words." She told my lawyer to be silent. I told her the story. When I was finished, she broke out laughing. Laughing. She really did. She told the troopers that they should have asked me why I waved them off and heard my side of the story. She sent me home and gave the troopers a reprimand. If they were angry when I arrived, they were raging furious when I left. You can bet that for the rest of our time in Leavenworth, I was one nervous driver. I would not have been surprised if they weren't just waiting for an opportunity to get back at me.
I never gave them the chance.

Some more recipes from the 1970's

# FISH PÂTÉ

This is a dish I made often in the 1970s. I made it again in the late 80's as part of the buffet for my friend Barbara's wedding. This is one dish that I think stands the test of time for taste. I now shy away from so much heavy cream and I have made it without the cream. Use the cream for richness and texture, but a low fat sour cream is an okay substitute. Just egg whites and no cream also works well. Over time I've have made adjustments and one I really like is a layer of cooked pureed peas. It is important to over flavor as it can be bland after it is cooked. Instead of sole try scallops…yummy.

| | |
|---|---|
| Sole fillets | 2 1/2 lbs. |
| Egg whites | 4 |
| Heavy cream | 1 3/4 cups |
| Salmon steak | 1 1/4 lb. (approx.) skinned, boned and cut into two strips |
| Cucumber | ½, peeled, scored and sliced thin |
| Lemon | 4 thin slices |
| Dill | 3 Tbsp. plus 1 sprig |

1. Remove bones from fillets and cut each fillet into 1" lengths.
2. Place one egg white and 1/4 of the fish in blender and blend on low until smooth. Remove to chilled bowl.
3. Repeat the blending process with all the fish and eggs. Cover the bowl and chill for about 1 hour.
4. Set the bowl of fish in a larger bowl with ice all around it. Gradually add a Tbsp. at a time, beat in the heavy cream so that it is absorbed before you add the next amount. You can use an electric mixer or a wooden spoon. This could take as long as 15 minutes.
5. Heat oven to 350 degrees.
6. Beat in 1/8 tsp. white pepper, 1/4 tsp. cayenne pepper and 2 1/2 tsp. salt, and the dill. (The level of seasoning can be checked by dropping a tsp. of the mixture into simmering water for two minutes. Do not taste uncooked.) 7. Butter a 9x5x3 loaf pan.
8. Spoon 1/2 half of the sole mixture into the pan. Arrange the salmon pieces lengthwise over the fish mixture, leaving a space between the two pieces.
9. Spoon the remaining fillet mixture over the salmon and spread evenly.
10. Cover with buttered parchment paper and set in a roasting pan with boiling water extended up the sides of the pan about 1/2 way.
11. Bake for 45 minutes or until loaf feels set when lightly touched. Chill.

Turn onto a serving platter and garnish with cucumber, lemon slices and dill.

I have also served this with a yogurt, dill and cucumber and horseradish mixture as a sauce.

# HUNTERS CHICKEN

Chicken stew, be it Italian, Greek or good old-fashioned American, has always been on my list. I do admit that, of the four of us, I was the only one who loved stew. Everyone else tolerated things all cooked together.

| | |
|---|---|
| Chicken | 1 3 1/2 lb., cut into pieces |
| Onion | 1 chopped |
| Red Pepper | 1 sliced in strips |
| Chicken broth | 1/2 cup |
| Red wine | 1 cup |
| Olives | 1 cup, mixed black and green without pits |
| Plum tomatoes | 1 28 ounce can with liquid |
| Garlic | 1 clove, minced |
| Flour | 1 cup (approx.) |
| Rosemary | 2 sprigs or 1/2 tsp. dry |
| Olive oil | 1/4 cup (approx.) |
| Parsley | 2 sprigs |
| Salt and pepper | |

PROCEDURE:

1. I remove the skin from the chicken. This is optional. Pat the chicken dry.
2. Season with salt and pepper.
3. Dip each piece of chicken in a small amount of flour to lightly cover.
4. Heat olive oil in large, heavy skillet and brown the chicken until slightly golden. Remove to a plate.
5. Sauté the onion, pepper and garlic.
6. Add the red wine, broth and the rosemary. Return the chicken back to the pan and heat until the chicken is cooked.
7. Add the olives.
8. Place the chicken on a platter.
9. Cook the sauce on high heat for 3 to 5 minutes until it is thick and the alcohol has burned off.
10. Pour the sauce over the chicken and sprinkle with fresh parsley.

Optional addition: mushrooms. I put mushrooms in anything possible. If using mushrooms, add them when you sauté the onion and pepper.

# CANNELLONI (another version)

This cannelloni is made with crepe batter and filled with meat. This is rich, filled with fat and calories. I can barely remember what this tasted like but rereading the ingredients, I do remember that the nutmeg is really important. With all those flavors and meat, protein and fat the nutmeg is the "high c "and makes the dish sing.

| | |
|---|---|
| Milk | 2 cups |
| Eggs | 6 |
| Flour | 1 cup plus 2 1/2 Tbsp. |
| Butter | 1/2 cup plus 2 Tbsp. |
| Olive oil | 1/4 cup |
| Salt pork | 4 oz. |
| Ground beef | 1 ½ lbs. |
| Italian Sweet Sausage | 1 lb. |
| Chicken Livers | ¼ lb. |
| Onion | ¾ lb. diced |
| Bay leaves | 2 |
| Garlic | 2, crushed |
| Parsley | 8 springs |
| Plum Tomatoes | 1 ½ lb. canned |
| Tomato paste | 1 Tbsp. |
| Spinach | 1 lb. |
| Parmesan cheese | 1/4 cup |
| Heavy cream | 1/4 cup |
| Nutmeg, salt and pepper | |

PROCEDURE:

Crepes:
1. Mix 1 cup water with 1 cup milk, 4 eggs and a dash of salt.
2. Add the 1 cup of flour and 1/4 cup of melted butter.
3. Cover and refrigerate at least 3 hours or overnight.
4. Using a 6" skillet, brush the pan with olive oil, and heat to very hot.
5. Place 2 Tbsp. of batter in the center of the pan and tilt the pan in all directions until the bottom is covered even to the sides.
6. Cook 60 seconds on one side the flip the crepe and cook for 30 seconds.
7. Remove to a plate and repeat with all the batter making about 12 crepes. Refrigerate until ready.

Meat sauce:
1. Combine 1/4 cup butter with olive oil and salt pork in a saucepan.
2. Add the onions and brown. Add the beef, chicken livers and sausage and bay leaves.
3. Cook slowly for 10 minutes.
4. Chop garlic and parsley and add to meat,. Cook 5 minutes.

5. Add the tomatoes. Cook for 30 minutes and the stir in tomato paste 6. Remove all the meat and grind. Return 1/2 the meat to the sauce.
7. Cook the meat sauce for 20 minutes.

Stuffing:
1. Steam the spinach and the drain and finely chop and then drain again.
2. Add 1/2 the meat mixture that was not used in the sauce.
3. Add 2 beaten eggs, cheese, nutmeg, salt and pepper.

Béchamel Sauce;
1. Stir 2 Tbsp. butter with 2 ½ Tbsp. flour in a saucepan over low heat.
2. Remove pan from the heat.
3. Boil 1 cup milk and add the boiling milk to the butter/flour.
4. Add pinch of nutmeg and slowly stir in the heavy cream. Heat on low until the sauce is thick. Remove from heat.

Assemble:
1. Place equal amounts of stuffing in the center of each crepe.
2. Fold crepe twice over the filling.
3. Arrange in buttered baking pan.
4. Spoon enough meat sauce over the crepes to cover.
5. Sprinkle 1/4 cup of grated cheese over the sauce.
6. Stir in 1/2 cup of the meat sauce into the warm béchamel sauce.
7. Mix well and spoon over everything.
8. Bake 350 degrees for 15 minutes. Serve with extra sauce.

# VEAL ORLOFF

This is a complex preparation with many steps but I love the combination of mushrooms, veal, and the soubise. I do not have notes where the original recipe came from. I am recording this from hand written notes but I know I did not make this up.

**For veal roast**

| | |
|---|---|
| tied boneless loin of veal roast | 1 (4 1/2-pound) |
| salt | 1 teaspoon |
| black pepper | 1/2 teaspoon |
| vegetable oil | 1 tablespoon |
| unsalted butter | 2 tablespoons |
| onion, finely chopped | 1 medium |
| celery rib, finely chopped | |
| large carrot, finely chopped | |
| fresh flat-leaf parsley | 6 sprigs |
| fresh thyme | 6 sprigs |
| bay leaf | |
| dry white wine | 1 cup |

**For soubise**

| | |
|---|---|
| long-grain white rice | 1/3 cup |
| unsalted butter | 2 tablespoons |
| onions halved | 1 lb.(3 cups), |
| salt | 1/2 teaspoon |
| chicken broth or water | 1/3 cup |

**For duxelles**

| | |
|---|---|
| mushrooms, minced | 1 pound |
| unsalted butter | 3 tablespoons |
| black truffles* (optional) | 2 tablespoons (1/2 ounce) finely chopped |
| heavy cream | 1/4 cup |
| salt, or to taste | 1/4 teaspoon |
| black pepper | 1/8 teaspoon |

**For Mornay sauce**

|  |  |
|---|---|
| whole milk | About 1 1/2 cups |
| unsalted butter | 4 1/2 tablespoons |
| flour | 6 tablespoons all-purpose |
| Gruyère | (1/3 cup) 1 oz. |
| salt | 1/2 teaspoon |
| black pepper | 1/8 teaspoon |
| nutmeg | 1/8 teaspoon |

Use a 5- to 6-qt heavy ovenproof pot;( I use a Dansk casserole that can go on the stovetop and in the oven. Now that I have an induction cooktop it works really well.) You will need cheesecloth; kitchen string;

PREPARATION:

**Braise veal:** Position oven racks in upper and lower thirds of oven and preheat to 325°F.

Pat veal dry and sprinkle with salt and pepper. Heat oil and 1 tablespoon butter in 5- to 6-quart pot over moderately high heat until foam subsides, then brown veal on all sides, turning with tongs, about 10 minutes. Transfer veal to a plate and discard fat from pot.

Melt remaining tablespoon butter in pot and cook onion, celery, and carrot over moderate heat, stirring and scraping up any brown bits, until softened, about 5 minutes.

Wrap parsley, fresh thyme (if using), and bay leaf in a square of cheesecloth and tie into a bundle with string to make a bouquet garni, then add to vegetables along with wine and dried thyme (if using). Put veal on top and bring to a simmer.

Cover pot with lid, then transfer to lower third of oven and braise veal until thermometer inserted 2 inches into center of meat registers 145°F, about 1 1/2 hours.

Transfer veal to a cutting board and let stand 30 minutes (internal temperature will rise to 155°F). Pour cooking juices from pot through a fine-mesh sieve into a 4-cup measure, pressing on and discarding solids. Skim off fat and reserve juices, adding any juices that have accumulated on plate from veal, for Mornay sauce.

**Make soubise while veal braises:** Precook rice in a large saucepan of **boiling salted water** 5 minutes, then drain in a sieve and rinse.

Heat butter in a 10-inch ovenproof skillet over moderately low heat until foam subsides, then stir in onions and salt. Cover tightly with a lid or a double layer of foil and cook onions over low heat, stirring occasionally, 5 minutes. Stir in rice and broth and bring to a simmer.

Cover skillet tightly, then transfer to upper third of oven and bake until rice and onions are very soft, about 1 hour. (Leave oven on.)

Transfer soubise to a food processor and pulse until coarsely puréed. Do not turn it into baby food. I like it with some texture. Transfer to a bowl to cool.

**Make duxelles while veal and soubise cook:** Put a handful of mushrooms in a clean kitchen towel (not terry cloth), then gather towel around mushrooms and wring them over sink to squeeze out as much liquid as possible. Wring out remaining mushrooms, a handful at a time, in same manner.

Heat butter in a 12-inch heavy skillet over moderately high heat until foam subsides, then sauté mushrooms and truffles (if using), stirring, until lightly browned and any liquid mushrooms give off is evaporated, 6 to 8 minutes. Stir in cream, salt, and pepper and cook, stirring, until cream is absorbed by mushrooms, about 1 minute. Transfer to a bowl and cool.

**Make Mornay sauce while veal stands:** Add enough milk to reserved veal juices to total 3 cups. Melt butter in a 2-quart heavy saucepan over moderately low heat, then add flour and cook over low heat, whisking constantly, 3 minutes. Add milk mixture in a stream, whisking, and bring to a boil, whisking. Reduce heat to low and gently simmer, whisking occasionally, 10 minutes. Remove from heat and add Gruyère, whisking until melted, then whisk in salt, pepper, and nutmeg.

**Assemble veal Orloff:** Move top rack to middle of oven and increase temperature to 375°F.

Stir 1/4 cup soubise into duxelles, then transfer remaining soubise to a sealable plastic bag. Transfer duxelles mixture to other sealable plastic bag, then seal each bag, squeezing out excess air. Snip off 3/4 inch from a bottom corner of each bag.

Remove string from veal, then trim off fat layer and ends of veal and discard. Cut roast crosswise into 16 slices (1/4 inch thick), keeping slices together. Transfer 1 slice of veal to end of ovenproof platter, then pipe about 1 1/2 tablespoons soubise onto half of slice, starting at bottom of slice and working toward top. Pipe about 1 1/2 tablespoons duxelles on other half of slice in same manner. Overlap with another slice of veal, leaving about 1/2 inch of stuffing exposed. Repeat with remaining veal slices and remaining soubise and duxelles, keeping slices aligned.

If necessary, heat Mornay sauce over low heat, stirring, until loose enough to spoon, then spoon 1/2 to 3/4 cup over top and sides of veal, covering slices and stuffing thinly but completely.

Bake veal Orloff, uncovered, until heated through and Mornay sauce glazes veal, 15 to 30 minutes.

Heat remaining Mornay sauce over moderate heat, stirring occasionally (thin with a little milk, if necessary), until hot and transfer to a gravy boat to serve on

## CHICKEN BREASTS WITH MUSHROOMS

This is a basic recipe and super easy. I have made it for years in different variations. I have served it with rice or noodles. I have also added sour cream or yogurt at the end to make the sauce a bit richer. In recent years the mushrooms have become more interesting as there is such a great variety at the markets. I love the flavor and texture they add to food.

| | |
|---|---|
| Chicken breasts | 3 boneless, skinless breast, cut in half |
| Olive oil | 3 Tbsp. |
| Butter | 2 Tbs. |
| Onion | 1 diced |
| Mushrooms | 1 lb. good quality mushrooms, sliced |
| Marsala wine | 1/2 cup |
| Chicken broth | 1 cup |
| Parsley, thyme | to taste |
| salt and pepper | to taste |

PROCEDURE:

1. Heat oil in a heavy skillet.
2. Brown the chicken in batches until each half breast is golden.
3. Remove chicken to heat proof platter.
4. Wipe the skillet clean and add 2 Tbsp. of butter.
5. Sauté the onion and then add the mushrooms. Cook until the cooking liquid has evaporated.
6. Add the Marsala and cook until it evaporates.
7. Add the broth and the herbs, reserving some of the parsley for later.
8. Simmer the sauce and add the chicken until it is tender.
9. Add 1 Tbsp. of butter and taste for seasoning.
10. Remove chicken back to platter, pour the mushroom sauce on top of the chicken and sprinkle with parsley.

# BAGELS

Living in Leavenworth Kansas in the 70's, there was not a bagel to be found. I am not sure that anyone had even heard of bagels and cream cheese with the Sunday newspaper. So one Saturday I made bagels for our Sunday breakfast. They were good but not great. I have been told that the secret to New York bagels is the water used for boiling the bagels. I am not sure of the veracity of that but bagels do seem to taste better the closer to New York you are. Maybe that is just childhood memories talking.

| | |
|---|---|
| Yeast | 2 packages, active dry |
| Flour | 4 1/2 cups |
| Sugar | 3 Tbsp. |
| Salt | 1 Tbsp. |
| Water | 1 1/2 cups lukewarm |

PROCEDURE:

1. In a large mixing bowl, combine yeast and 13/4 cups of flour.
2. Combine water, sugar and salt.
3. Add to yeast mixture.
4. Beat in a mixer at low speed for 1/2 minute. Scrape the sides of the bowl and continue to beat at high speed for 3 minutes.
5. Gently stir in the rest of the remaining flour to make a stiff dough.
6. Put dough on floured surface and knead until smooth, about 6 minutes.
7. Cover and let rest about 15 minutes.
8. Cut the dough into 12 portions and shape into smooth balls
9. Punch a hole in the center of each with your finger that has been dipped in flour.
10. Pull gently to enlarge the hole. (this is one cooking experience that is helped by being a potter)
11. Make each bagel in the same manner.
12. Cover for about 20 minutes to allow them to rise.
13. In a large pot, boil 1 gallon of water with 1 Tbsp. of sugar.
14. Reduce the temperature to simmering and add the bagels.
15. Cook for 7 minutes turning once. ( you may need to cook in batches)
16. Drain.
17. Place on greased baking sheet and bake 375 degrees for 15 minutes.

You can add any seasonings to the dough prior to boiling and seeds to exterior prior to the baking.

## BROWN RICE, RYE, MILLET AND KIDNEY BEANS

Not yet vegetarians but trying to take "healthy cooking" seriously, this is an example of two of my attempts.

| | |
|---|---|
| Kidney beans | 1/2 cup. Soaked overnight and cooked until tender (or use good quality canned beans) |
| Millet | 1/2 cup |
| Brown rice | 1/2 cup |
| Rye | 1/2 cup (you can substitute any other grain) |
| Onion | 1 chopped |
| Garlic | 1 minced |
| Parsley | 2 sprigs, chopped |
| Tomatoes | 1 large can, drained |
| Cheese | 1/2 cup, grated |
| Vegetables | any assortment, diced and steamed. i.e: zucchini, mushrooms, peas, carrots |

PROCEDURE:

1. Cook the grains in 4 cups of boiling water until they are tender.
2. Add the cooked beans.
3. Sauté the onion and garlic and add to the grains.
4. Add the tomatoes and vegetables.
5. Put in a casserole and cover with cheese.
6. Bake until hot and the cheese is melted.

Suggestion to spice it up: use chili powder mixed with 2 Tbsp. tomato paste.

# RICE AND VEGETABLES, ASIAN INSPRIED

This shows up at the end of the 70s and a good example of where our diet was moving. A big change from Veal Orloff and Beef Wellington.

| | |
|---|---|
| Brown Rice, long grain | 2 cups |
| Onion | 1 chopped |
| Carrots | 3 peeled and diced |
| Chinese cabbage (Napa) | 1 cup, sliced |
| Spinach | 1 lb., chopped |
| Snow peas | 1 cup |
| Bamboo shoots | 8 oz. |
| Water Chestnuts | 8 oz. |
| Bean sprouts | 1 cup |
| Tofu | 1 lb. |
| Ginger | 2 or 3 slices, minced |
| Garlic | 1 clove, minced |
| Soy sauce or soy bean paste to taste | |
| Cornstarch | 1 Tbsp. |
| Lemon juice | 1 lemon |

PROCEDURE:

1. Cook in a large skillet 2 cups of rice in 4 cups of water.
2. Sauté chopped onion, ginger and then garlic (do not burn the garlic).
3. Add the water chestnuts and bamboo shoots. Check for oil so vegetables crisp and do not burn.
4. Add the sliced cabbage and spinach and cover. Cook slowly. Check if you need to add a bit of water. It should cook without water as the cabbage and spinach produce liquid.
5. Add snow peas, bean sprouts, and tofu. Cook until all the vegetables are heated.
6. Mix the 1 Tbsp. of cornstarch with 3/4 cup of water. Add soy to taste. Stir in the lemon juice and pour over the vegetables. Mix to well blended. Taste for seasoning.
7. Add vegetables and rice to a serving platter. The vegetables can be mixed into the rice or placed on top.

## FROZEN CRANBERRY-PINEAPPLE SALAD

This recipe is SO 70s! When I found this index card in my file, I remembered how good I thought this was. I remember the time I made it…our last Thanksgiving in Minneapolis (early 1970). What a contrast from my Julia Child cooking. This was a hit. I guess compared to jello molds it was unique.

| | |
|---|---|
| Cream cheese | 2 small packages |
| "Miracle whip" | 2 Tbsp. |
| Heavy cream | 1 cup whipped to soft peaks |
| Pineapple | 1 can crushed pineapple |
| Cranberry sauce | 1 can whole cranberries |
| Walnuts | Chopped (a small handful) |

PROCEDURE:

1. Mix all the ingredients together.
2. Line a loaf pan with parchment or wax paper.
3. Pout the mixture into the pan.
4. Freeze.
5. When ready to serve, unmold on to a platter. Slice with a serrated knife.

# LEMON SQUARES

Reading a recipe for Lemon Squares may not seem like a big deal, but when I first discovered them they were. When we were living in Leavenworth. A' neighbor told me about a party she went to were they served a cookie bar where the filling tasted like the middle of a lemon pie and the top was confectioners sugar. We both searched cookbooks (if there was the Internet, the search would have taken a minute rather than days). I finally found a recipe that matched her description and now people were asking me for the recipe for these delicious bars. I think my source was the *New York Times* but now all I have is a small index card where some of the ink is smeared (must have gotten wet).

Shopping List:

| | |
|---|---|
| Flour | 2 cup |
| Butter | 2 stick |
| Confectioners sugar | 1/2 cup plus extra for topping |
| Eggs | 4 |
| Sugar | 2 cups |
| Flour | 4 Tbsp. |
| Lemon Juice | 1/4 cup |
| Baking powder | 1 tsp. |

PROCEDURE:

1. Mix flour, butter and confectioners sugar.
2. Pat in the bottom of a 13x9" pan.
3. Bake 350 degrees for 15 minutes.
4. Beat the eggs and sugar until fluffy.
5. Add the flour, baking powder and lemon juice to the eggs.
6. Pour the egg mixture on top of the baked crust.
7. Bake 325 degrees for 20 minutes.
8. Sift confectioners sugar over the top.
9. Cool and cut into squares.

## CHOCOLATE RASPBERRY CAKE

| | |
|---|---|
| Cocoa | 1 cup |
| Flour | 2 1/2 cups |
| Baking soda | 2 tsp. |
| Baking powder | 1/2 tsp. |
| Salt | 1/2 tsp. |
| Butter | 1 cup |
| Sugar | 2 1/2 cups |
| Eggs | 4 |
| Vanilla extract | 1 1/2 tsp. |
| Chocolate chips | 1 bag |
| Raspberry puree | 1 jar |
| Framboise or kir | 1/4 to 1/2 cup |

Fresh raspberries and whip cream (optional)
Chocolate ganache or frosting (optional)

Spring form pan, buttered and floured

PROCEDURE:

1. Dissolve cocoa in 2 cups of boiling water. Cool.
2. Sift the flour, soda and powder and salt together.
3. Beat the sugar and butter together until fluffy.
4. Add the eggs and vanilla to the butter/sugar.
5. Alternately add the cool cocoa, flour mixture and egg/butter in a large mixer bowl.
6. Beat until smooth.
7. Add the chocolate chips.
8. Pour mixture into prepared spring form pan.
9. Bake in 350 degree oven for about an hour.
10. Cool and then cut the cake into three layers.
11. Heat the preserves with the liquor.
12. Frost each layer with the raspberry glaze.
13. The cake can be served plain or with fresh raspberries and whipped cream. Or cover the exterior with your favorite chocolate frosting.

## DOBOSCH TORTE

I was surprised when I came across this recipe in my handwriting on a dirty piece of lined paper. Dirty from cooking stains means I made this cake, and I am sure more than once. I made a lot of flavored whipped cream desserts. One terrific one with ladyfingers and ground almonds that can be found in *Mastering the Art of French Cooking*. It is a Charlotte: strawberry or chocolate. I must have made this quick dessert when time was short. If you are looking for real "homemade," skip Sara Lee and make your own wonderful pound cake.

SHOPPING LIST:

| | |
|---|---|
| Pound cake | 1 store bought, frozen (Sara Lee…if it still exsists) |
| German sweet chocolate | 4 oz. |
| Coffee | 1/4 cup brewed (decaf okay) |
| Cognac | 2Tbsp. |
| Heavy cream | 1 1/2 cup |

PROCEDURE;
1 Cut frozen pound cake into 6 layers.
2. Melt chocolate in coffee.
3. Stir in cognac.
4. Whip cream.
5. Fold into chocolate.
6. Frost each layer and the top.
7. Chill at least 1 hour until serving. Overnight is fine.

PIES: I loved making pies starting with my first one in my mother-in-law's kitchen in 1962, and I continue to try to perfect them today. Besides the classic fruit, there was a period of time where pies were made with the ingredients of favorite cocktails. The following two pies were company pleasers while we lived in Minneapolis

## BRANDY ALEXANDER PIE

| | |
|---|---|
| Gelatin, unflavored | 1 envelope |
| Sugar | 2/3 cup |
| Eggs | 3, separated |
| Cognac | 1/4 cup |
| Crème de cacao | 1/4 cup |
| Heavy cream | 2 cups, whipped |
| Graham cracker crust 9" | |
| Chocolate curls for garnish | |

PROCEDURE:

1. Sprinkle the gelatin over 1/2 cup of water in a saucepan. Add 1/3 cup of sugar, 1/2 tsp. salt and 3 egg yolks.
2. Heat the gelatin mixture over low heat while stirring until gelatin dissolves and the mixture thickens.
3. Remove from the heat and stir in the liquors. Chill the mixture until soft set.
4. Beat the 3 egg whites until stiff. Gradually beat in the sugar and fold into the thickened mixture. Fold in 1 cup of the whipped cream. Turn into the prepared crust. Chill several hours.
5. Garnish with remaining whipped cream and chocolate curls.

## **GRASSHOPPER PIE**

SHOPPING LIST:

| | |
|---|---|
| Chocolate wafer cookies | 8 oz. |
| Sugar | 2/3 cup |
| Butter | 4 Tbsp. |
| Gelatin, unflavored | 1 envelope |
| Eggs | 3 separated plus 1 egg white |
| Heavy cream | 2 cups |
| Green Crème de menthe | 3 1/2 Tbsp. |
| White Crème de cocoa | 4 1/2 Tbsp. |
| Cream of tartar | 1/8 tsp. |
| Vanilla | 3 Tbsp. |
| Confectionary sugar | |
| Chocolate curls | 3 Tbsp. |

PROCEDURE:

1. Crush wafers and combine with 1 tsp. sugar and 4 Tbsp. butter. Line 10" pie plate and bake for 10 minutes.
2. Sprinkle gelatin over 1/2 cup of water in saucepan. Add 1/3 cup of sugar, 1/8 tsp. of salt and 3 egg yolks. Stir while heating until thickened. Remove from the heat.
3. Stir in the liquors and refrigerate until cool (about 15 minutes).
4. Beat the 4 egg whites with the cream of tartar and a dash of salt until stiff. Gradually add the remaining sugar. Fold into the cooled mixture.
5. Combine heavy cream with vanilla and confectionary sugar and whip the cream.
6. Fold the whipped cream into the mixture and pour into the piecrust.
7. Chill. Decorate with chocolate curls.

The similarity in these two recipes was never so obvious to me when I was making them. Now I see there is a formula and you can flavor it any way you choose. My new challenge is to bring this concept to the flavors of the 21$^{st}$ century.

## PUMPKIN FLAN
A nice change from pumpkin pie.

SHOPPING LIST

| | |
|---|---|
| Sugar | 2/3 cup |
| Eggs | 2 plus 3 yolks |
| Sugar | 6 Tbsp. |
| Pumpkin puree | 1 cup |
| Light cream | 1 1/2 cups |
| Orange liqueur | 2 Tbsp. |
| Cinnamon | 1 tsp. |
| Ginger | 1/4 tsp. |
| Nutmeg | 1/8 tsp. |
| Cloves | 1/8 tsp. |

PROCEDURE:

1. Heat a 6 cup soufflé dish in a pan of hot water.
2. In a heavy skillet cook 2/3 cup of sugar with 3 Tbsp. of water.
3. Cook the mixture until it is golden caramel.
4. Pour the caramel into the heated dish, turning to cover the bottom
5. In a , beat 2 eggs plus 3 yolks and 6 Tbsp. of sugar until foamy.
6. Beat in pumpkin puree, all the spices plus 1/2 tsp salt.
7. Gradually stir in scalded light cream and the orange liqueur.
8. Pour into caramelized dish.
9. Put dish in pan of hot water so that the water comes up 2/3 sides of the dish.
10. Bake 350 degrees for 1 1/4 hours.
11. Invert on serving platter and serve with orange liqueur flavored whipped cream.

# MARBLEHEAD, MASSACHUSETTS
1973-1997

Back of house after our second remodel.

Front of the house. Remodel done in the 90's. This is a view of the new deck and the sitting room off the kitchen.

The two years in Kansas came to an end too quickly. They were a great two years, but it was time to start our "real" life. Joe was starting his medical practice in Salem, Massachusetts. I was getting my master's degree and working part time in the Marblehead Public schools. Jonathan and Wendy started school in Marblehead. We bought our first home, a large beautiful house owned by the bank and us. It was a central entrance, colonial sitting on top of a small hill a mile from the Atlantic Ocean, but it no longer had water views. The house was built in 1912 and the street was then called Oceanview. It was now called Longview Drive, as trees and hundreds of houses between our home and the ocean changed the views. I always thought the name change clever, someone had a good sense of humor.

The 1912 kitchen was remodeled in the 40's and now needed some updating. We were about to do our first kitchen.

Kitchen (Butler's Pantry) just as we are ready to take the sledge hammers to it.

We gutted the space. The original kitchen became a small family room and the butler's pantry was converted to the kitchen space. The wall that separated these two rooms was gone and now we had the perfect spot for our table. The table connected the cooking to the sitting space. We did most of the work ourselves with the help of some graduate students from MIT. None of us had ever done anything like this, but we had a vision. The cabinets were butternut. They were a beautiful warm golden brown. I wanted the doors to be one piece of wood with no molding, design or any stylizing. They were stunning for about a month until they started to warp. The counters were to be butcher block, but we could not afford the commercially made butcher block so me made our own. They looked great as long as we kept on top of repairing the seams that would open from moisture. The piece of marble that was inserted in the counter for baking was a stroke of genius. We included three pull-out waste bins so all the recycling was hidden and efficient. Yes, Marblehead was recycling even then. A large food pantry was another great feature. But the single most noticeable part of the kitchen, the thing that gives it time (1970's) and place (New England) was the basket collection that hung from almost every inch of the wood ceilings.

Some of the baskets were collectables and some less dear, but they all had a story—where they were found or what they were used for. The white ironstone pitchers and platters and my blue and white plate collection were everywhere. Old metal kitchen implements hung on their own small wall. It was fun collecting all that stuff. We would comb Maine and New Hampshire for treasures. I now have three of those baskets. I gave my daughter most of the plates but still have much of the ironstone. I loved that kitchen.

This was our vegetarian period. Joe was slowly moving in this direction towards the end of our years in Minneapolis. His personal research about heart disease, which was a strong concern with his family's history, led him to believe that fat and especially animal fat had to be eliminated from our diet. At first I felt so betrayed. I grew up eating kale and cabbage salad and baked potatoes. I had learned to cook and love meat, chicken, cheese and bacon. How could he do this to me?

What was stronger than my desire to eat meat was my respect for Joe's intelligence and I really believed that he was right, so I slowly embraced a new way of eating and cooking. I learned to make some creative and edible dishes. Many of them were my own inventions, but I was also a regular user of the Moosewood cookbooks.

It was in this kitchen while we are serious vegetarians that I was photographed for my first and only publicity as a cook. A reporter and a photographer came to our home to interview me. It was a profile of a "vegetarian cook." The fact that I lived and worked in Marblehead, I am sure that word of our eating habits filtered to someone who wrote for the local paper. So the appointment was set: I was interviewed and they took photos of my Brown Rice and Tofu dish, which on that day contained every vegetable that was available on the Eastern Seaboard. It was artfully arranged on an Arabia plate. The fish platter is a tofu loaf meant to taste and look like fish with grapes and flowers decorating the sides (to distract the viewer from what the food is?). The platters were on my wood counter and my basket collection was hanging over my head. When I look at photos, I laugh at the thought of what a 70's stereotype we ended up being in our efforts to be individuals. We kept failing at being "one of a kind."

What's with the hairdo? It looks like a helmet, but I would give anything today to have enough hair to do that. It was always fine but now it is thin! So as I aged, my hair got thinner and my waist got thicker!

That kitchen saw countless small dinner parties, large cocktail parties and even a wedding. My friend Barbara got married at our house and I was pleased and proud to do all the cooking for more than 80 people. My white ironstone platters were filled with food that I had been preparing for weeks. Thank goodness for a large freezer in the basement.

It was in this kitchen that we established some cherished memories and some not so cherished. MooShu pancakes were one of our fonder food memories. The four of us made this dinner together. We made the pancakes using Joyce Chen's recipe and filled them with mushrooms, tiger lily and cabbage. We made hot and sour soup and stir-fried some vegetables to put on top of brown rice. We believed this was better than any local take-out, except we never did make fortune cookies.

Sitting space: looks like a fruit and veggie party…hmm. Note the pharmacy scale. You had to put a penny in to weigh yourself.

This looks like a family Thanksgiving. (fake flowers!)

Kitchen facing the back yard

**TWO TOFU RECIPES**

Tofu, in my opinion, is tasteless, but it is a perfect canvas for anything. During the peak of our vegetarian cooking, I used it instead of cheese in Lasagna. I would puree a block of tofu with an egg white, nutmeg, parsley and black pepper. I would do the same with the spinach and ricotta recipes. The following are a few examples of tofu gone sort of elegant. These recipes have a strong Asian influence but do not be limited to those flavors. Substitute tofu for veal in your favorite scaloppini recipes. Tofu Marsala works. It is wonderful addition to Eggplant Parmesan. Alternate the layers of eggplant with slices of tofu and bake.

### Carrots, Swiss chard and Tofu:

| | |
|---|---|
| Swiss chard | 1lb. shredded |
| Tofu, firm | 1 lb. cut into cubes or slices |
| Carrots | 2 cup julienne |
| Red pepper | 1 thinly sliced |
| Shallot | 1 thinly sliced |
| Ginger | 1 Tbsp. chopped |
| Lemon juice | 1 lemon |
| Oil | 1 Tbsp. (I have used sesame oil and olive oil) |
| Low salt soy sauce | to taste |

Cooked brown rice
Toasted sesame seeds to taste

PROCEDURE:

1. Steam the Swiss chard and carrots until they are softer than raw but still have a "bite."
2. Sauté the shallot and red pepper.
3. Add the ginger, tofu, carrots and Swiss chard and stir until all the ingredients are hot.
4. Add the lemon juice and soy to taste.
5. Serve with brown rice and toasted sesame seeds.

## Tofu Noodle Soup

| | |
|---|---|
| Dark sesame oil | 1 Tbsp. |
| Firm tofu | 12 oz. |
| Bok choy | 6 cup chopped |
| Carrots | 2 diced |
| Shitake mushrooms | 6 sliced |
| Ginger | 1 Tbsp. chopped |
| Soba noodles | 3 cups, cooked |
| Low salt soy | 1 Tbsp. |
| Cilantro | 1/2 cup chopped |

Broth:

| | |
|---|---|
| Water | 6 cups |
| Onions | 1/2 cup |
| Carrot | 1/2 cup |
| Dried shitake mushrooms | 1/2 cup soaked in hot water |
| Ginger | 3 thin slices |
| Low salt soy | a splash |
| Garlic | 1 clove |

PROCEDURE:

1. Make the broth by cooking the carrot, onion and mushrooms in the water and the mushroom soaking water. Add the soy, ginger and garlic.
2. Simmer the broth for 30 minutes. Strain out the solids.
3. Add the tofu, bok choy, carrots, mushrooms, ginger and noodles to broth.
4. Heat gently until all the ingredients are hot.
5. Add the soy to taste and the cilantro.

## VEGGIE BURGERS TWO WAYS

### LENTIL BURGERS

| | |
|---|---|
| Lentils | 1 1/2 cup |
| Rolled oats | 1/2 cup |
| Garlic | 1 minced |
| Coriander | 2 Tsp. ground |
| Cumin | 2 Tsp. |
| Egg | 1 beaten |

PROCEDURE:

1. Cook the lentils about 20 minutes until they are soft but not mushy. Drain the lentils.
2. Grind the oats into a meal.
3. Combine the lentils, 3 Tbsp. oats and spices. Mash the ingredients with the back of a large spoon.
4. Stir in the egg.
5. Form into 6 burgers.
6. Coat the burgers with the remaining oats and chill for 15 minutes.
7. Brown in a skillet about 4 minutes on each side.
8. I served them with yogurt and mint but ketchup, lettuce and tomato works.

### NUT AND GRAIN BURGERS

| | |
|---|---|
| Cracked wheat | 2 cups |
| Soy Flakes | 1 1/2 cups |
| Barley | 3/4 cup |
| Water | 7 cups |
| Onion | 1 chopped |
| Pecan | 3/4 cup ground to a meal |
| Tamari, garlic, pepper taste | |

PROCEDURE:

1. Cook the cracked wheat, soy flakes and barley in the water.
2. Sauté the onion and add to the grains.
3. Add the seasonings and the pecan meal. Taste for seasoning.
4. Shape into patties and heat in the oven until hot.

r.

## LENTIL PÂTÉ

| | |
|---|---|
| Lentils | 1 1/2 cups |
| Onion | 1 diced |
| Garlic | 1 minced |
| Parsley | large bunch, chopped |
| Stale bread | 3 slices, soaked in water |
| Coriander | pinch |
| Celery seed | pinch |
| Chili powder | pinch |
| Fresh dill | 2 Tbsp., chopped |
| Egg | 1 beaten |
| Lemon juice  Salt and pepper | 1/2 lemon |

PROCEDURE:

1. Cook the lentils in water until they are tender.
2. Sauté the onions and garlic in olive oil.
3. Add the chopped parsley.
4. Squeeze out the water from the bread and add to the onion, garlic and parsley.
5. Add the seasonings and cook for about 10 minutes.
6. Add water if it gets too dry.
7. Put the lentils in the food processor with the onion, egg and lemon juice and blend the mixture.
8. Bake in a prepared (greased or parchment paper) loaf pan for 30 minutes at 350 degrees.
9. It can be served hot or cold.

# MAC AND CHEESE

I think a painting of Jello goes well with Mac and Cheese.

| | |
|---|---|
| Elbow macaroni | 1lb. |
| Butter | 6Tbsp. |
| Flour | 6 Tbsp. |
| Mustard | 2 Tbsp. |
| Milk | 6 Cups |
| Onion | 1 small, diced |
| Paprika | 1 tsp. |
| Cheddar cheese | 1 ½ Cups |
| Parmesan cheese | 1 Cup |
| Bread crumbs ( Panko) | |

PROCEDURE:

1. Cook the macaroni until tender. Set aside.
2. Sauté the onions until soft.
3. Melt the butter. Add the flour and whisk until well blended.
4. Very slowly add the milk while you continue to whisk. I heat the milk first.
5. Add the diced cooked onion to the thickened milk.
6. Add all the cheese and taste for salt and pepper.
7. Mix the macaroni and cheese sauce together in a large casserole.
8. Sprinkle the top with breadcrumbs.
9. Bake 350 until it is bubbling hot. Check in one half hour.

## MANDARIN PANCAKES (for Moo Shi)

This Chinese pancake recipe is from the *Joyce Chen Cook Book*. Joyce Chen had a wonderful Chinese restaurant in Cambridge, Massachusetts. The pancakes are easy to make and can be made in advanced. Don't let the long directions mislead you. Once you make them, you see the logic to each step. If you cook your rice in a rice cooker, which you should, you can reheat the pancakes in the steamer tray in the rice cooker.

| | |
|---|---|
| flour | 1 3/4 cup |
| water | 3/4 cup boiling |
| sesame oil | 2 tsp. |

1. Mix the flour with the boiling water in a bowl with a wooden spoon.
2. As soon as your hands can stand the heat, knead the dough until it is smooth, for about 3 minutes.
3. Cover with a wet towel and set aside for 1/2 hour.
4. Form the dough with your hands into a cylinder.
5. Roll it on a lightly floured board and make it a strip exactly 12" long.
6. Cut the roll (use a ruler) into 1" sections.
7. Stand each of these sections on the end and roll them between the palms of your hands into round cylinder.
8. Flatten the cylinders into round cakes.
9. Brush one side of each cake evenly with sesame seed oil.
10. Put one cake on top of another. Oil sides together. Flatten the two cakes smoothly with the heel of your hand.
11. Roll the 6 pairs of cakes into 6 flat thin pancakes. Roll uniformly so they are the same size and thickness. They should be about 7" in diameter.

1. Use an ungreased skillet (crepe or omelet pan is ideal) or a grill pan also works well.
2. Medium low heat.
3. The cakes take less than one minute to get light brown spots (do one at a time). Turn and cook about 1/2 minutes on the other side.
4. Pull the cakes apart so you now have two thin pancakes. The six pairs will be 12 thin pancakes.
5. Keep the pancakes covered so they do not dry out.
6. I sometimes put waxed paper between the cakes so when I steam them, they stay dry. Do not let them touch the water when you steam them.
7. If you are using a regular pot for rice make sure you wrap the pancakes in foil if you are going to put them on top of the rice.

## MANDARIN MOO SHI FILLING

The filling can be any recipe of vegetables, pork, chicken or seafood. The following recipe is based on Joyce Chen's, with my variations.

| | |
|---|---|
| Lean pork | 1/2 cup cooked and shredded |
| Dried wood ears | 1/4 cup (black fungus is another name) |
| Golden needles | 1/2 cup (Tiger Lily) |
| Eggs | 4, beaten |
| Dry sherry | 1 tsp. |
| Soy sauce | 2 Tbsp. |
| Corn starch | 1 tsp. |
| Oil | 3 Tbsp. |
| Ginger root | 1 slice |
| Scallion | 1 shredded |

My list:
We were making these pancakes during our veggie period, so no pork, but more vegetables.
Instead of pork we used
Shredded cabbage
Bean sprouts
Mushrooms
We did not use the 4 eggs either. We have made it with egg whites and like it just as well. Never use MSG and with the soy sauce and the commercially made hoisin sauce we served with the pancakes there was enough salt for us.

PROCEDURE:

1. Pour boiling water over the wood ears, cover and soak for 15 minutes.
2. Do the same with the tiger lilies.
3. Mix the pork or the vegetables with the sherry, soy sauce and cornstarch.
4. Heat 2 Tbsp. oil and cook over medium heat.
5. Add the diced ginger.
6. In a separate pan, scramble the eggs and then add to the cooked mixture (pork &/or veggies).
7. Add the scallion, wood ears, tiger lily, stirring constantly.
8. Mix well and serve with the pancakes and the rice you needed to cook so you could steam the pancakes.

Italian cooking was always a win-win in our house, except for my quick and easy English muffin pizzas and the pizza I made with a shredded zucchini crust. All the failures were not mine, however. Joe became infamous for his oatmeal dinner.

My husband has come such a long way from this disaster and is now a really good cook but it has taken years for our children to forgive and forget this fiasco.

Joe loves oatmeal. Our morning routine was to get up at 5 a.m. (this is only when the children were old enough for us to leave the house…no child neglect) and go to a nearby Jewish Community Center to swim 1/2 mile, shower and dress for work. When we got home, I would wake the children and help them get organized while Joe made oatmeal. Not everyone ate oatmeal every morning, but it was always there as an option. Anyway, the real story is that Joe had seen me make polenta and had this great idea of what to do with all the oatmeal that no one ate for breakfast. He put it in a loaf pan and chilled the loaf. That evening he cut the cooked, chilled mush into slices and baked them. He made a sauce and some vegetables and surprised us with dinner. Joe loved it and still remembers that dinner fondly.

I think our biggest success with food and family time had to be Taco Sunday. We had an enormous platter? Bowl? Sculpture? Thing. It was yellow, plastic and at least 2 1/2 feet round. On one side it looked like different shaped craters of the moon, on the other side it looked like planets in a fictional universe. When the bowl was not in use, it hung on a wall in the basement, but on many Sundays it sat on the round coffee table in the living room in front of the fireplace.

Its wells were filled with ingredients for "make your own taco." We had shredded iceburg lettuce, chopped tomatoes, cucumber, olives and avocado, beans, cheese, sour cream and salsa.

It was not just the food that was fun. It was sitting on the floor and making a mess. The dynamics were always better. When we bought our cabin in Maine, the bowl moved up there and was filled with a wide variety of pick up foods or was hanging on the wall as art.

Gourmet dinner groups became very popular and, rolling with the current, we joined one. We were not all friends and had little in common except cooking and the enjoyment of meeting new people, not unlike our Minnesota experience. No one was a vegetarian and we were starting to be more flexible. We ate poultry and fish socially and would nibble at meat. We knew it is always a positive experience to enrich our lives with people whom we would not have had an opportunity to meet any other way. Our group had only a few rules: pick a country and divide up the menu. The food had to be authentic to the country. It had to be made with all fresh ingredients and take way too long to prepare. One dinner that left a lasting impression on me was at our home. The country, Germany, was not a cuisine I favored or knew much about. I found an interesting soup. The stock of the soup was beer and the recipe gave instructions on how to make the beer. Not one to shy away from a challenge, two weeks before the dinner, I started the beer. I'm now trying to come up with the word to describe the taste of that soup. No one had more than one small taste before it went down the garbage disposal, followed by a lemon to get rid of the awful smell. The entree I made was Hasenpfeffer (rabbit stew), which redeemed my credibility, but was never made again.

Another dinner, also at our home: the menu was food from Russia. We started with shots of vodka and caviar. We took a bottle of vodka and divided it into smaller bottles, flavoring each differently. Coffee bean is one I remember. I got blotto that night, the night we were drinking shots. I know I got the rest of the dinner to the table and I know that we had a good time, but it is all a hazy fog. The trouble is that everyone was in the same state, so no one can recall much of that night. We all remember the next morning. The funniest part of that evening was that my parents were visiting from New York and were happy to join in the pre-dinner drinking. They both fell asleep on the living room floor and never made it to the dining room. They both snored through our evening and didn't seem to mind that they missed the foods of their ancestors.

Our central entrance colonial house was a perfect layout for holiday celebrations. We had many Thanksgivings: some with my extended family from New York, some with Joe's from Springfield and a few times with everyone. We always tried to include some non-family guests, particularly single physicians who were on call and not able to travel to family. Finding themselves in our family dynamic, I often wondered if they might have preferred the hospital cafeteria. They always seemed to treat our idiosyncratic behavior with humor, but doctors in training are good at pretending to care.

The idiosyncratic behavior of our family could sometimes be thought of as funny and other times aggravating. One of Joe's brothers insisted that we always sit at a round table for easy conversation—for sure a good idea, but not always possible. I am sure my need to have everything organized annoyed some and others where just glad it was me and not them doing all the work.

One Thanksgiving I was getting the large casserole of hot mashed potatoes out of the oven. The oven rack was not secure and the pot heavy. Within seconds I had steaming hot mashed potatoes burning my chest and abdomen. Talk about chaos! The days of putting butter on a burn were over. Now the thought was ice cubes. I was in acute pain. Joe was at first in a panic, but quickly slipped into doctor mode. After ten minutes of pain. I was ready to eat a dinner with ice cubes on my belly.

Jewish holidays also became an important focus for us. Since our children had no formal religious training and were growing up in a secular Jewish home, we felt that the observing of major holidays would give them the important historical and symbolic relevance of their inherited faith. I grew up in a secular home but I was proud to be Jewish. It was important that our children understand what it meant to be Jewish. Both of our children have continued their Jewish heritage with their children. On Yom Kippur, the Day of Atonement, we had a private ritual. It was always just the four of us. We would often take a walk on the beach and then share something we had done during the year that might have hurt the feelings of someone. The goal was that we would each reach out to someone we had slighted. Joe always did it. He made a phone call. The rest of us were less brave and only rarely did it. Sometimes we would be invited to "break the fast" with friends, but if we were alone we usually had kugel (noodle pudding). The biggest deal was Passover. We used stories written by friends and edited by us to include folk music. The service was not traditional but the message was as old as the original intent and the food was classic. We looked forward to that dinner: gefilte fish with beet horseradish, haroset (walnuts, apples, cinnamon and red wine), matzo ball soup, roast chicken, green beans and roasted potatoes. The desserts were made without flour, which meant for us lots of egg whites, whipped cream and chocolate. We loved sharing this celebration with friends and family. It was always a time of thought provoking conversations.

Once we had another venue for sharing holiday celebrations with other families. Through word of mouth and someone who knew someone who knew someone else, we formed a group of families who wanted to expose their children to the concepts of all the major faiths. They were looking to be part of a community, but not belong to a Church or Temple. Our mutual goal in forming the group was to create an experience for the children. The adults started meeting at night to make plans for what we wanted to do with our children, but before we knew it we were talking about relationships and our emotional lives. We were twelve couples. Our goal was for our children to have a spiritual experience with other families. It didn't take long to realize that most of the others were struggling with something much more complex in their relationships. It was obvious that many of their marriages were being held together by nothing stronger than habit. There was the moment when one of the woman, angry most of the time, starting attacking every man in the room. Joe and I were horrified at how mean she was and saddened to see her husband disappear into his chair. By the end of the two years, the group was no longer satisfying for anyone and within a few years only two couples were still married. It was the 80's and divorce was in the air. Before all the marriages fell apart, we did manage to have a day where the focus was our kids. It was a beautiful winter Sunday at our home and all our families were introduced and told about the plans for the day. Early in the morning, Joe and Larry went to the woods and dug up a birch tree that would eventually get replanted. The tree, in a pot, was put in our "garden room." This room was a step down from the living room with a flagstone floor, two walls of windows, a piano and too many plants.

The house was organized into "work groups" (kids and adults). One group went to the basement and made a piñata. Another group was in the dining room making ornaments for the tree and the third group was in the kitchen making potato pancakes. When the preparations were completed, we went outside to break the piñata. Teens and toddlers smashed apart the homemade piñata filled with candy. Photos show a group of adults standing around and a bunch of kids with "now what?" expressions.

So that was okay but not a huge success. Next stop…Christmas. We decorated the tree and we had enough piano players for a long enough carol sing-a-long so the cooks could get the meal on the table and get ready for Hanukah.

We lit the candles. Told the shorten version of the story and then filled our plates with potato pancakes and an abundance of food from casseroles made by each family. All the kids were good sports, but there was no real bonding. The group continued for two years but had nothing to do with religion or creating a community for our children. Some of the couples sent their kids to religious school, some did nothing and some continued, as we did, an attempt to do it alone. For us that meant observing, in our own way, the major Jewish holidays, and most likely too many discussions about being a "good person."

All our years in Marblehead were not just about food. Joe had a demanding medical practice, did clinical research and made sure that none of us felt short changed. In his rare spare time, he built Shaker style furniture, more beautiful, I have to say, then my father's colonial pieces that were falling apart.

We cross-country skied, rode bikes, hiked and tried to keep our kids a part of our lives for as long as we could. We were also lucky to take four overseas trips with Jonathan and Wendy. The first trip was to England. Jon was 11 and Wendy was 9. It was a first for all of us as we had never been out of the United States. We learned a great deal about history, their culture, the people we met and the new foods we ate but the best part was that we learned we could travel together. There were none of the little annoyances that happen at home. So two years later we rented a house in Israel to celebrate Jonathan's thirteenth birthday. We were there for a month. We still talk about how that trip was an adventure and an amazing experience. We met some interesting people, one who lived in Haifa and visited us twice in Marblehead. We ate food we loved. Every moment we learned something about the culture of the Middle East, the Jewish diaspora, and that the politics and the ancient story are so entwined. Two years later when Wendy was thirteen she chose France. Not a bad choice! Our last trip together, when they were both in college, was to Portugal. Just like our other trips we rented a car and drove everywhere. Since this is a story about food…Portugal and Greece were my favorite food countries. Fresh fish and vegetables prepared to perfection! Our trip to Greece was done when Jon and Wendy were not available. Jon was in a bike race in Ireland and Wendy was working at a camp in the Berkshires. We rented a car and I think we saw every corner of the country plus an Island. I look back and think how fortunate we were to have these trips and to do them in a way that was fitting our life style: small

B&B's, cafes and poking around neighborhoods. We of course also made sure we saturated ourselves with the culture and the energy of the cities.

I did digress with this short travel log. I wanted to let you know my life was more than just food, but of course it was also always about food. Besides the cooking and travel and the outdoor stuff I did work, and I loved my job.

I worked in the public schools in a job that had many hats. I was a guidance counselor, meeting with individual students, groups of students, and lots of parents. Health educator: teaching sex-ed, drug and alcohol awareness, nutrition and all the other things that go into being a healthy human being. Special education chairperson: IQ testing, assessing other tests done by a myriad of specialists and most importantly meeting regularly with teachers and parents in the hopes that a plan and program was designed to meet the student's needs and the parents' expectations. Through my twenty plus years, I worked at every level but middle school was my favorite. I found that age group fun and challenging. I know middle school doesn't sound like fun, dealing with all the issues of self-esteem and puberty, but that is what I liked. One day a student would act like a young child with a need for a hug. The next day the same student would be walking with an air of self-confidence and an attitude of "I don't care what anyone thinks". They are at an age where they are learning to reason and think for themselves but not too old to admit that they need help. There were lots of challenges but never a moment where I didn't feel that I had the possibility to make a difference. I may not have made that kind of difference often but when I did it counter balanced all the times I struck out. I still had to be on guard not to be manipulated for, despite all the training and experience, I was still the gullible 20 year-old once manipulated by a prison inmate. Because of Facebook I am in touch with many of those students who are now much older than I was when I first screened them for kindergarten.

At the end of everyone's busy day, we all met in the kitchen. Our gathering place was a classic oak claw foot round table. "All Things Considered" on the radio did not seem to be a distraction: I couldn't cook without it. Not to make this sound too "Leave it to Beaverish," (there were arguments and there were bad moods, and there were times when everyone was in their own rooms with the door shut), but this is my memoir and the memories I choose to hold on to were those times that it was perfect. And even if they were rare, they are remembered. As you are picturing this scene don't forget to add the lazy chocolate lab, Hershey. She was always there except when she was too lazy to move from the last place she had fallen asleep. Elky had been run over by a police car shortly after we moved to Massachusetts and replaced by Hershey, another example of naming brilliance! Chocolate lab…Hershey! We should have gone with something more elegant like Godiva.

During these years, and still today, our politics never changed. We still believed in civil rights for everyone and equal opportunities for health care and education.

We served on boards, voting for the "right" (or should I say left) causes, but did not go the next step. We had friends who stood in front of nuclear power plants with signs, marched on Washington, traveled to South American and Cuba and were much noisier than we were. We signed the petitions but didn't knock on other people's doors.

What we did is give our children our same values and watched them become the kind of citizens that express our values. Our professional lives, in education and medicine, gave us opportunities to give on a small scale to the community we served. So we talked the talk but we didn't always walk the walk, but we did try. I could be outspoken at work and was known to stand my ground on issues that I felt passionate about. Joe was the same. We took turns over the years in being in the middle of battles with administrators over the welfare of a student or a patient. But day-to-day we were a suburban couple raising two children in a beautiful home in an exquisite town. It took effort to remind ourselves that most people did not live as we did.

This kitchen, home to all this togetherness, after many years got tired and we had moved on from being "hippies" to yuppies. We kept moving further and further away from those early years in Roxbury. The warped cabinets and splitting counter had lost their charm. Brown rice and tofu were boring and the baskets dusty. Sledgehammers in hand, this place of memories was demolished in a weekend. This was a family affair. Each of us had a section of the wall, a big hammer and masks to try to protect us from the dust. It all went down way too fast. We thought it was going to be a weekend project, but we were ready for the building crew in less than a day.

We had beautiful white custom-made cabinets with glass doors and true divided lights. The counters were dark green, almost black, granite. This was when the idea of granite was still new and questionable but I had seen it in Eva's kitchen, a neighbor and friend, and it made perfect sense. The quarry tile floor, which was hard on the legs and impossible to clean, was now replaced with wood. The sitting room was converted back to the kitchen space and the kitchen was now an enlarged sitting space that opened to a new deck that looked out at our flower, herb and vegetable gardens. New windows and a French door brought this space to the point of luxury. Fabulous appliances and more cabinets than anyone needs. A buffet with a cherry counter softened the coldness of the granite and became home to some of my favorite collections. Dating back to my second kitchen in 1964, I still believed that there should be a cabinet to show off prized pottery and glass collections.

Jonathan and Wendy's high school graduation parties had been held in the country kitchen of their childhood. The basketball court was used for rented tables and chairs. By the time we had the new kitchen and gardens (the basketball court was now an herb garden), they were both at college and fewer family memories were made in the sleek and shiny new space.

Our new kitchen

Scale is gone. The sitting spot with books is now a pantry.

The rocking chair is the first piece of furniture we bought back in 1964. It had been in a fire and was charred black. When cleaning it up, we discovered mother of pearl inlay and lovely wood. It squeaked…great for nursing babies. Coffee table used to be a kids wagon. Aunt Mildred did the needlepoint pillow. We bought the rugs from friends who owned a import rug store in Beacon Street in Boston. Couch and chair, Crate and Barrel.

Marblehead Gardens (and my really blond hair…I didn't think I ever had it that light. Must be the sun!)

Herb Garden that use to be the basketball court.

## SUGARLOAF MAINE

Marblehead is a peninsula surrounded by a harbor and the Atlantic Ocean. The harbor is so packed with sailboats that you can almost walk from one to the other without getting your feet wet. Sailboat racing was the preferred sport and yacht clubs dotted the shore. Not sailors or yacht club members, we spent our weekends in the mountains of Maine and New Hampshire. After years of camping, renting cabins and staying at charming inns, we bought a wonderful cabin on the Carrabasett River near Sugarloaf Mountain, Maine. The cabin had one large room, two small bedrooms and a sleeping loft. The kitchen was separated from the living space by a bar. The stove was a camp stove, the water came from the river and the heat came from a wood-burning stove. In the winter we skied (cross country for us and downhill and cross country for the kids), and in the summer, spring and fall there were endless hiking and canoeing adventures. Food in the mountains always tasted better: pancakes, pasta and popcorn. We entertained ourselves with games, books and conversation. No television and everyone was forced into one room. It worked, most of the time. Everyone was usually so tired from the day's activities that chilling out together was easy.

**SUGARLOAF** (the river side of the cabin. That is Joe heading to the frozen river)

Sugarloaf Kitchen

Note the bottom half of yellow "taco bowl" on the wall

In the 90's, we started to think about retirement plans and thought about buying something more substantial in Maine. We drove over to the other side of the mountain to Rangeley Lake and found a wonderful big old house: no heat, lots of bedrooms and baths and a big old-fashioned kitchen. The house was on the lake on a beautiful 2 acre piece of property. It was perfect. We had just finished the remodel of the Marblehead kitchen and loved the contrast of this country farmhouse. We brought all our old collectables and put them in this new kitchen. I made slipcovers for the furniture (the house came furnished) and curtains and bedcovers—all challenging my sewing skills. Our ten-year plan to fix up Marblehead had taken over twenty years, and that was done. Now we had our retirement home and a year later **WE SOLD IT ALL!**

# RANGELEY, MAINE

The house we thought we would live in once we retired….

Rangeley Kitchen

The perfect houses did not answer the restless feeling that Joe and I both had. The children grown and making their own lives, we felt like our dedication to our work was waning and we needed a change and new challenges.

A hospital opportunity in Greensboro, North Carolina fit Joe's professional ambitions and the South would certainly meet the criteria of something new. The new job would be an administrator at a large well-respected hospital and health care system. It was a teaching hospital. Joe would be wearing many hats but one was to facilitate the setting up of a cancer center. I didn't have a job yet but was in no hurry to find one. We had a lot of work to do, remodeling a house and figuring out how to become part of a new community.

After Joe made rounds for the very last time at Salem Hospital, we hit the road.
It was a bleak, gray Christmas day and we had the road to ourselves. Scared and excited, we left 28 years behind us and headed south without looking back.

A few more recipes from the 1980's

## LENTIL CASSEROLE

Lentils become an important ingredient when you are not eating meat or poultry. We all enjoyed classic lentil soup but I was always looking for other ways to use lentils. They really can be the canvas for so many preparations. I liked them with the warm spices of cumin and coriander so this casserole was a natural fit.

| | |
|---|---|
| Lentils | 1 cup |
| Celery | 2 ribs cut into large pieces plus 2 cups diced |
| Carrot | 2 cut into large pieces |
| Onion | 1 cut into large chunks plus 2 sliced |
| Zucchini | 2 cut into cubes |
| Leeks | 2 cleaned and cut into slices |
| Garlic | 2 minced |
| Parsley | 3 springs |
| Thyme | 2 tsp. |
| Coriander | 3 Tbsp. fresh |
| Cumin | 1 tsp. |
| Black pepper | |
| Yogurt | 1/2 cup plain |

PROCEDURE:

1. Cook the lentils in 2 1/2 cups of water with the 2 celery ribs, 2 carrots and the 1 onion. Add 1 parsley and thyme.
2. Boil the water and then reduce to simmer, cover the pot and cook about 30 minutes.
3. Remove the cooked celery, onion and carrot. Add the diced vegetables (leeks, zucchini and celery.
4. Cook uncovered over medium heat for about 15 minutes. Taste for tenderness..
5. Heat 2Tbsp. olive oil in ovenproof Dutch casserole. Sauté the onions, garlic for about 10 minutes. Stir in the lentil mixture and reduce the heat to low.
6. Chop the remaining parsley and coriander.
7. Add the coriander, parsley, cumin and black pepper to taste. Slowly add the yogurt.
8. Bake until hot.

# PASTA SAUCES

During the 80's, the most popular food in our diet was pasta in every form. The favorite with my family was the traditional tomato sauce, but to give some variety I would try different presentations. They were all greeted with nods of acceptance but never as a replacement for the classic.

## ROASTED TOMATO SAUCE

| | |
|---|---|
| Roma tomatoes | 1lb. cut in half |
| Onion | 1 cut into wedges |
| Fennel | 1 cut into wedges |
| Red pepper | 1 cut in half and seeded |
| Garlic | 1 clove or to taste |
| Black olives | 1/4 cup, pitted |
| Basil | 1 bunch, fresh |
| Parsley | 1 bunch, fresh |
| Olive oil | |
| Salt and pepper | |

Lightly oil the bottom of a roasting pan. Place the tomatoes, onion, fennel and red pepper in the pan
Roast at 450 degrees until they are soft.
Put all the ingredients in a food processor. Use short, quick "on and off" until everything is chopped.
Warm sauce but do not over cook. It is served at room temperature in Italy.

## WILD MUSHROOM

Mushrooms: An assortment of wild and cultivated mushrooms. Amount should be at least a pound.
> I love mushrooms. You can use dried mushrooms that are soaked in hot water. Use that water for the sauce.

| | |
|---|---|
| Olive oil | 2 Tbsp. |
| Cognac or Marsala | 1/2 cup |
| Evaporated skim milk | 1 small can |
| Parsley and pepper | to taste |

Sauté the sliced mushrooms in the oil. Add the cognac and cook down. Stir in the milk and season with chopped parsley and black pepper.

## WHITE BEANS AND SUN DRIED TOMATOES

| | |
|---|---|
| Onions | 1 cup, sliced |
| Garlic | 1 Tsp., minced |
| White Cannellini beans | 2 cans, drained |
| Sun dried tomatoes | 1 cup, quartered |
| Thyme | 1 tsp. |
| Basil | 1 Tbsp. fresh, 1 tsp. dried |
| Salt and pepper | |
| Parsley | |

Sauté the onion and garlic. Add the rest of the ingredients until heated. Use with penne pasta. Not great with spaghetti.

## GREENS AND PINE NUTS

| | |
|---|---|
| Pine nuts | 1/4 cup, chopped |
| Onion | cut into wedges |
| Garlic | 1 minced (or to taste) |
| Olive oil | 2Tbsp |
| Thyme | 1tsp. |
| Greens | 2 lbs. coarsely chopped (spinach, Swiss chard, kale) |
| Broth | 3/4 cup (vegetable or chicken) |

Brown nuts in 400 degree oven until golden. Watch carefully. This happens fast. Roast the onion, garlic in oil and thyme in 400 degree oven for 25 minutes Add the greens and roast another 10 minutes.
Add the pine nuts, salt and pepper and add to cooked pasta.

# CAPONATA

This is my "go to" appetizer. I make it all the time, knowing that if there are any leftovers it is good in sandwiches or on top of pasta. I always served it with crackers but on some occasions I borrowed an elegant idea from *The Natural Cuisine Of Georges Blanc*. This a beautiful recipe/photography book. Mr. Blanc suggests serving caponata as a filling for smoked salmon. Take a slice of smoked salmon, place a Tbsp. of caponata at the end and then roll the slice. Serve with lemon. This recipe for caponata is not from any cookbook. Over time it has evolved to this simple preparation.

| | |
|---|---|
| Eggplant | 1 large globe, peeled and cubed |
| Celery | 2 stalks including the leaves, sliced |
| Onion | 1 diced |
| Olive oil | enough to generously cover the bottom of the skillet |
| Balsamic vinegar | 1 Tbsp. |
| Sugar | 1 Tbsp. (optional) |
| Tomatoes | 1 14 oz. can of diced. I like Fire Roasted tomatoes |
| Green Olives | 1/3 c. pitted and sliced |
| Black olives | 1/3 c. pitted and sliced |
| Capers | 2 Tbsp. . |
| Black pepper | |
| Parsley | |

PROCEDURE:

1. Sauté the onion and celery in olive oil in a large skillet.
2. Add the eggplant and continue to cook until all the vegetables are coated with some olive oil.
3. Add the vinegar and stir until everything looks browned by the vinegar.
4. Add the sugar and mix well.
5. Add the tomatoes, lower the heat and cover the skillet.
6. Cook for about 10 minutes, checking regularly, and stir so nothing sticks to the bottom of the pan.
7. Add the olives and capers and continue cooking until all the vegetables are soft and the liquid is absorbed.
8. Taste for seasoning. Add pepper and parsley. I do not add salt because the olives and capers add salt. You may find it needs to be salted.
9. Chill for at least a few hours or overnight.

# SHRIMP AND SCALLOP RECIPES

## SHRIMP, ARTICHOKES AND FENNEL

| | |
|---|---|
| Jumbo shrimp | 16 |
| Artichoke hearts | 1 can or 8 saved from fresh artichokes |
| Rosemary | 1/4 tsp. |
| Garlic | 2 cloves |
| Fennel | 2 bulbs |
| Thyme | 1/4 tsp. |
| Lemon juice | 1/4 cup |
| Olive oil | 4 Tbsp. |
| Red pepper flakes | 1 tsp. (to taste) |

PROCEDURE:

1. Combine the rosemary, garlic and 2 Tbsp. of oil.
2. Add the shrimp and turn to well coated. Marinate for 30 minutes..
3. Mix 2 Tbsp. of oil with red pepper flakes, salt, pepper. Pour over the artichoke hearts and bake for 15 minutes.
4. In saucepan combine the fennel, thyme, and lemon juice. Stir in 1/3 cup of water. Cover and simmer over low heat for 20 minutes.
5. Prepare a grill or heat the broiler. Grill or sear the shrimp until they are pink (2 to 3 minutes on each side).
6. Add shrimp and artichoke hearts and fennel to bowl.
7. Season with lemon juice, oil, salt and pepper.
8. Serve over pasta.

## SCALLOPS AND FIGS

I like sweet food and this is an example.

Make sure you get DRY Scallops with no preservatives. These are the only ones that caramelize nicely.

| | |
|---|---|
| Marmalade (orange or ginger or a mixture) | 3 Tbsp. |
| Shallots | 1/4 cup, chopped |
| Marsala wine or sherry | 2 Tbsp. |
| Red pepper | 1/2 tsp. |
| Garlic | 1 clove, chopped |
| Scallops | 1 LB |
| Dried Figs | 8 Oz. |
| Lemon | 1 |
| Olive oil | 1 Tbsp. (approx.) |

PROCEDURE:

1. Mix the marmalade, shallots, wine, red pepper and garlic together.
2. Pour mixture in a plastic bag and add the scallops and figs.
3. Marinate in the refrigerator for about 1/2 hour.
4. Remove the scallops and figs and put the marinade in a small saucepan.
5. Sear the scallops and figs.
6. Cook the marinade, adding a small amount of water if needed so it makes a glaze.
7. During the last minute of cooking add the glaze to coat the scallops and figs.
8. Serve with rice or couscous.

## SHRIMP WITH FETA CHEESE

| | |
|---|---|
| Medium Shrimp | 2 lbs. |
| Onion | 1 chopped |
| Garlic | 1 or more to taste (chopped) |
| Lemon juice | 1 lemon |
| Olive oil | 1/2 cup |
| Parsley | 1/2 to 1 cup, chopped (I use more rather than less parsley) |
| Crushed tomatoes | 1 large can. Use a really good quality |
| Tomato paste | 1 to 2 tsp., depending on desired thickness |
| Cognac(or wine) | 1/4 cup |
| Oregano or mint | 1 tsp. You can use both…I do. |
| Fennel seed | 1/2 tsp., crushed. (Optional) |
| Feta Cheese | 3/4 lb., crumbled |

PROCEDURE:

1. Dry shrimp and marinate in the lemon juice.
2. Heat oil is a large skillet (I like one with high sides) Add the onions and garlic. Sauté until the onions are soft
3. Add the cognac, tomatoes, tomato paste, oregano, herbs and the juice from the canned tomatoes. You may need to add a small amount of water.
4. Cover and simmer for about 20 minutes. Check for thickness and if water is needed.
5. Oil a baking dish and preheat the oven to 375 degrees.
6. Mix the shrimp in the sauce and then add all the ingredients to the baking dish.
7. Put the feta cheese on top and bake for about 20 minutes, when cheese starts to melt.
8. Serve with orzo or any other pasta or rice.

# SEAFOOD PAELLA

You can use almost any seafood. When I first started making most of my company dishes or celebratory family dinners with seafood, when we lived in Marblehead, it was not hard to find a wide variety of fish and it was not outrageously expensive. Now, after years on the west coast and back on the east coast and still eating a lot of fish and seafood we try to buy local fish and fish that is sustainable. In the 80's, that was not on my radar screen.

| | |
|---|---|
| Saffron | 1/4 tsp. |
| Firm fish fillets | 1 lb., cut into 2" pieces |
| Shrimp | 8 to 10 extra large in the shell |
| Squid | 10 oz., cleaned and cut into 1" pieces |
| Clams or mussels | 1 lb. |
| Paprika | 1 Tbsp. |
| Tomatoes | 4 diced. Do squeeze out the liquid. |
| Garlic | 1 or to taste, minced |
| Red pepper | 1 chopped |
| Onion | 1 small, chopped |
| Fish broth** | 7 cups |
| Rice | 2 1/2 cups short grain |

PROCEDURE:

1. Soak the saffron in 1/4 cup of hot water and let it rest for 15 minutes.
2. Season the fish filets with salt and pepper.
3. Heat a 16 to 18 paella pan (I recently bought a paella pan. In the 80's and up until recently I used a very large fry pan.)
4. Add the shrimp and fish fillets and cook until golden brown. Set them aside.
5. Add the squid, paprika, tomatoes, garlic, peppers and onions to the pan and cook until the onions are soft. Add the saffron mixture and broth and bring to a boil.
6. Add the rice and distribute the rice.
7. Reduce the heat and add the fish and put in the clams, pushing them down under the rice so they cook.
8. Cook about another 10 minutes.
9. Cover with foil and let sit for a few minutes before serving.

**If you do not have a fish stock, I use a combination of bottled clam juice and white wine. I have seen recipes use a chicken stock. You just want to have more depth to the stock than water.

# SOFT POLENTA WITH MUSHROOM SAUCE

One of my food passions is mushrooms. (I think I have said that more than once). When I crave comfort food, it is often sautéed mushrooms with one of the following: covering a baked potato, and stuffed into the skin and eaten like a sandwich, in an omelet, or on top of pasta. The seasoning that I think works the best with mushrooms, besides salt and pepper, is thyme. If the dish has mushrooms, I almost always add a bit of thyme. Marsala wine adds depth and a bit of sweetness.

| | |
|---|---|
| Polenta cornmeal | 1 1/3 cup |
| Salt | 1/2 tsp. |
| Olive oil | 2 Tbsp. |
| Assorted wild mushrooms | 1 lb. |
| Butter | 2.Tbsp. |
| Shallots | 4 Tbsp. |
| Thyme | 1/4 tsp. |
| Parsley | 2 Tbsp. |
| Marsala or sherry | 1/2 cup |
| Tomato paste | 1 Tbsp. |
| Parmesan cheese | |

PROCEDURE:
1. To make polenta: place 5 cups of water and salt in large saucepan and bring to boil. Whisk in the polenta very slowly, whisking continually to prevent lumps. Lower the heat and, with a wooden spoon, continue to stir until the polenta is very thick…about 20 minutes.
2. To make the sauce:
    1. Clean and slice the mushrooms.
    2. Using a large sauté pan add the oil and butter.
    3. . Sauté the shallots and then add the mushrooms.
    4. Add the sherry and cook until most of the liquid is evaporated.
    5. Add the tomato paste and the thyme and parsley.
    6. Optional to add a bit more butter or some hot water to make the sauce the consistency you want.
    7. Serve the soft polenta with the mushrooms sauce and pass the cheese.

## SPINACH TORTE

This is a quick and easy recipe and nothing about it is unusual. It is just a great stand by with ingredients that are easy to have on hand. Note the similar ingredients in the 1960's Spinach Roll. I always like nutmeg in baked spinach dishes.

| | |
|---|---|
| Spinach | 1 lb. fresh or frozen |
| Ricotta cheese (non-fat for us) | 1 lb. |
| Onion | 1 medium, chopped |
| Red pepper | 2 chopped |
| Mushrooms | 1 lb. fresh, sliced |
| Eggs or egg whites | 3 or 4 |
| Nutmeg, salt and pepper to taste | |

PROCEDURE:

1. Fresh spinach: steam and drain dry.
2. Frozen spinach: do not cook. Defrost and drain dry.
3. Sauté the onion and mushrooms until soft.
4. Beat the eggs until blended.
5. Now this is the hard part: mix all the ingredients together. Taste for seasoning.
6. Put it in a prepared pan. Pan options: spring form, loaf pan or a square-baking dish. The shape of the pan will determine how it is served: Square pan means you will cut the spinach in small squares, a loaf pan means slices. Prepare the pan with cooking oil, or what I like is to use parchment paper.
7. Bake in 350 degrees until firm (about 1 hour).
8. Serve with Parmesan cheese or a simple tomato basil sauce.

# ZUCCHINI "CHARLOTTE"

I named this dish "Charlotte" since it resembles in shape the wonderful whipped cream dessert made with ladyfingers. Instead of lining the pan with ladyfingers, this vegetable dish uses zucchini. The attached photo was taken in Greensboro, North Carolina but the first time I made this dish was in the 70's in Marblehead.

Overly busy counter ruins the effect but you can get the idea.

| | |
|---|---|
| Tomatoes | 1 to 2 lbs. |
| Eggplant | 1 large globe |
| Zucchini | 2 lbs. (about 5 zucchini) |
| Onion | 1 small |
| Garlic | 1 clove |
| Red pepper | 1 |
| Olive oil | |
| Thyme | |

1/2 loaf of Italian or French bread
Salt and pepper

A mandoline makes this dish easier to prepare. It is difficult to cut the zucchini thin enough without one. I have a very inexpensive mandoline and never understood why I would need an expensive one. It works fine.

PROCEDURE:

1. Chop the tomatoes and eggplant, pepper and 2 zucchini in cubes.
2. Dice the onion.
3. Slice the bread and lightly toast it. Rub the bread with garlic.
4. Heat enough olive oil to cover the bottom of a large sauté pan.
5. Sauté the onion, eggplant, pepper and the 2 zucchini until they are soft and dry.
6. Cook the tomatoes long enough for them to soften but not lose their shape.
7. Mix all the vegetables and tomatoes together. Season to taste.
8. With the mandoline, slice the remaining zucchini lengthwise into strips.
9. Blanch the zucchini for 2 minutes just so they are soft enough to bend.
10. Line a round mold or bowl (I use my Charlotte pan, but any bowl with a diameter of 9" will work.)
11. Place the zucchini slices around the bowl so the tips meet at the bottom and slices overlap.
12. Fill the mold with the vegetables alternating layers with the bread until you fill the bowl. Cover with foil.
13. Place bowl in a cooking pan with enough hot water to fill halfway up the sides of the bowl.
14. Bake 350 degrees for about one hour.
15. Invert the bowl and unmold on a platter.
16. I serve it with a light tomato sauce and cheese.

# CHICKEN WITH GREEN SAUCE
A nice summer dish. The chicken is served cold.

Broth:

| | |
|---|---|
| White wine | 1 cup |
| Onion | 1 small, chopped |
| Carrot | 1 chopped |
| Celery | 1 chopped |
| Tarragon | 2 tsp. |
| Parsley | 2 tsp. |
| Peppercorns | 6 |
| Chicken breasts | 6 whole, cut in half |

| | |
|---|---|
| Spinach | 1 cup |
| Watercress | 2 Tbsp. |
| Tarragon | 2 tsp. |
| Shallots | 1 chopped |
| Lemon juice | 4 Tbsp. |
| Vinegar, white | 2 Tbsp. |
| Mustard | 1 Tbsp. Dijon is best |
| Olive oil | |
| Avocado | 2 |

PROCEDURE:

1. Mix the broth ingredients together in a large pot. Simmer the broth for about 20 minutes.
2. Add the chicken and simmer for 20 minutes.
3. Remove the chicken and cool.
4. The broth can be frozen and saved for another use.
5. The sauce: mix the spinach, watercress, tarragon and shallots in a food processor.
6. Add 1 Tbsp. of the lemon juice, vinegar and mustard and enough olive oil to make a smooth sauce.
7. Salt and pepper to taste.
8. Slice the cooled chicken and the avocado. Pour the remaining Tbsp. of lemon juice on the avocado.
9. Pour half the green sauce over the chicken and serve the rest of the sauce in a bowl.

# PASTILLA

Tofu can be substituted for the chicken, and vegetable broth for the chicken broth. The texture will not be the same, but you will get the wonderful Moroccan flavors. This is NOT really low fat because of all the eggs. But each person really is only eating 1 egg as it makes 8 to 10 wedges.

| | |
|---|---|
| 2 chickens | 2 1/2 lb. to 3 each |
| Oil for cooking | 3/4 cup (sesame oil adds a great flavor) |
| Ginger | |
| Paprika | |
| Cumin | |
| Coriander | 1 tsp. of each spice |
| Turmeric | |
| Pepper | |
| Cinnamon stick | 1 |
| Chicken broth | 1 quart |
| Saffron | 1 tsp. |
| Raisins or currants | 1 cup |
| Onion | 3 cups finely chopped |
| Sesame seeds | 1/4 cup toasted |
| Whole almonds | 1 cup blanched |
| Confectioners sugar | 1/2 cup |
| Cinnamon | 2 tsp. |
| Lemon juice | 1/4 cup |
| Eggs | 10 |
| Butter | 3 Tbsp. melted: Use sparingly to brush each leaf |
| Phyllo dough | 12 leaves (approx.) |
| Salt and pepper | |

PROCEDURE:
1. Brown the chicken in 1/2 cup oil
2. Combine the spices and the cinnamon stick and sprinkle over the chicken.
3. Cover the pot and cook for about 15 minutes.
4. Heat the broth. Remove from heat. Add the saffron and let steep 5 minutes.
5. Add broth to chicken. Cover and cook for 1 hour.
6. In a skillet, heat 3 Tbsp. of oil and cook the onions. Stir in the currants and sesame seeds.
7. Brown the almonds in 1 Tbsp. of the oil. Remove and pat dry. Cool and grind to a powder. Add sugar and cinnamon
8. Remove the chicken from the pot. Boil the liquid until it reduces to 1 ¾ cups. Add enough lemon juice to make 2 cups.
9. Shred the chicken and add 1 cup of broth, salt and pepper.
10. Boil remaining broth.
11. Beat the 10 eggs and pour into the boiling broth. Stir for about 15 minutes. The eggs should make a solid mass with all the liquid absorbed.
12. Assembling:

1. 12" SKILLET or a 4 QUART BAKING DISH
2. Wrap phyllo leaves in a damp towel and use 1 leaf at a time.
3. Brush each leaf with butter as you use them.
4. Use 6 leaves to line the bottom and the sides evenly overlapping.
5. Cover the bottom leaves with the almond, cinnamon sugar mixture
6. Combine the chicken and eggs and put on top of the almonds.
7. Layer the onion/currants on top of the chicken.

Bring the sides of the leaves over the top. Cover the top with the six remaining layers, tucking the overhanging layers inside the pan.

Bake 400 degrees for 20 minutes.
Loosen the sides.
Pour off excess butter.
Invert on a baking sheet.
Bake 400 degrees for 10 to 20 minutes to hot and brown.
Sprinkle with sugar, cinnamon and sesame seeds.

Cut in pie shaped wedges.
I usually serve it with a salad

# MUFFINS

I was surprised how many muffin recipes I collected. I know there were brunches, but neither Jon nor Wendy were big muffin lovers and Joe would eat them if they had no fat and were filled with healthy stuff. I liked them but would not have made them just for myself. I did, on occasion, bring some to work and have some in the freezer…in case. So I guess I kept collecting and baking muffins for no apparent reason.

I am not going to bore you with all of these recipes, but am going to include a few: some that are super healthy and some that just taste good.

## WAY TO START YOUR DAY MUFFINS

Combine the following ingredients:

| | |
|---|---|
| Flour | 1 cup |
| Shredded bran cereal | 1/2 cup |
| Toasted wheat germ | 1/2 cup |
| Rolled oats | 1/2 cup |
| Cornmeal | 1/2 cup |
| Sugar | 1/2 cup |
| Chopped walnuts | 1/2 cup |
| Raisins | 1/2 cup |
| Baking powder | 2 tsp. |
| Baking soda | 1 tsp. |
| Cinnamon | 1 tsp. |
| Ginger | 1/2 tsp. |
| Nutmeg | 1/2 tsp. |

Mix the following together and add to the flour/cereal mixture

| | |
|---|---|
| Buttermilk | 1 cup |
| Butter, melted | 1/3 cup (or oil) |
| Apple, chopped | 1 |
| Egg | 1 beaten |

Pour into prepared muffin tins and bake 25 minutes at 400 degrees.

**OAT PEAR MUFFINS**

Combine the following:
| | |
|---|---|
| Fine ground rolled oats | 2 1/2 cup Can |
| unsweetened pears | 16 oz. |

*Reserve the juice and put in a measuring cup*
*Add enough:*

| | |
|---|---|
| Skim milk so the liquid measures | 1 cup. |
| Brown sugar | 1/3 cup |
| Egg whites, beaten | 2 |
| Vanilla extract | 1 tsp. |
| Chopped walnuts (optional) | |

Put in prepared muffin tins and bake 350 degrees for 20 minutes.


**GINGER PEAR MUFFINS**

I love ginger so it does not surprise me that many of my collected recipes have ginger as a major ingredient.

| | |
|---|---|
| Dried pears | 4oz. |
| Ripe pear | 1 |
| Flour | 2 cup |
| Baking powder | 2 tsp. |
| Baking soda | 1/2 tsp.. |
| Salt | 1/2 tsp. |
| Nutmeg | 1/2 tsp. |
| Eggs | 2 |
| Sugar | 2/3 cup |
| Milk | 1/2 cup |
| Vanilla extract | 1 tsp. |
| Butter, unsalted | 1/3 cup |
| Candied ginger, chopped | 3/4 cup |

PROCEDURE:
1. Soak dried pears in boiling water for 15 minutes. Dry and chop.
2. Peel and core fresh pear. Chop into same size pieces (about1/2").
3. Mix all the dry ingredients.
4. Whisk the eggs, milk, vanilla and butter with the pears.
5. Add the ginger and mix the wet and dry ingredients together.
6. The batter should not be over mixed. Lumpy is okay.
7. Put in prepared muffin tins.
8. Bake 400 degrees for about 20 minutes.

## APRICOT PEACH MUFFINS

| | |
|---|---|
| Dried apricots | 6oz. |
| Can peaches, unsweetened | 16 oz. (save the juice) |
| Flour, white | 3/4 cup |
| Flour, whole wheat | 3/4 cup |
| Baking soda | 1 tsp. Baking |
| powder | 1 tsp. |
| Cinnamon | 1/2 tsp. |
| Sugar | 1/4 cup |
| Egg whites | 2 |
| Vanilla extract | 1 tsp. |

PROCEDURE:

1. Finely chop the peaches and the apricots.
2. Mix dry ingredients then add the egg whites, sugar, vanilla and fruit and the reserved juice.
3. Bake 350 degrees for 20 minutes.


## CRANBERRY ORANGE MUFFINS

| | |
|---|---|
| Egg whites | 4 |
| Sugar | 1 ½ C. |
| Lemon juice | 1 Tbsp. |
| Orange rind | grated from 1 orange |
| Skim milk | 1 cup |
| Flour | 2 1/2 cup |
| Baking powder | 1 Tbsp. |
| Baking soda | 1/2 tsp. |
| Salt | 1/2 tsp. |
| Cranberries | 2 cups chopped |

PROCEDURE:

1. Beat the egg whites with mixer until frothy.
2. Add the sugar and continue to beat 1 minute.
3. Stir in lemon juice, orange rind and skim milk.
4. Add the flour, baking powder and soda and mix by hand until moist.
5. Fold in the cranberries.
6. Spoon into prepared muffin pan.
7. Bake 400 degrees for 20 to 30 minutes.

## LEMON DATE PECAN MUFFINS

| | |
|---|---|
| Brown sugar | 1/2 cup |
| Butter, unsalted | 6 Tbsp. |
| Lemon juice | 5 Tbsp. |
| Honey | 1/4 cup |
| Sour cream | 1/2 cup |
| Egg | 1 |
| Lemon peel | 1 Tbsp. grated |
| Flour | 1 3/4 cup |
| Baking powder | 1 12 tsp. |
| Baking soda | 1/2 tsp. |
| Dates, chopped | 1 cup |
| Pecans, chopped | 2/3 cup |
| Salt | 3/4 tsp. |

PROCEDURE:

1. Cook sugar, butter, lemon juice and honey until heated and dissolved.  2. Whisk sour cream, egg, lemon peel to blend. Add cooled sugar/butter
3. Combine dry ingredients and then add to liquid to blend.
4. Add dates, pecans and 1/4 cup of hot water. Mix. It will be lumpy.
5. Bake 400 degrees for 20 minutes.

# NUTS FOR APPLECAKE
This is also good not so nutty.

| | |
|---|---|
| White sugar | 1 1/2 cup |
| Brown Sugar | 1/2 cup |
| Vegetable oil | 1/2 cup |
| Eggs | 3 whole eggs, or 6 egg whites for lower fat |
| Flour | 2 cups |
| Salt | 1/4 tsp. |
| Baking powder | 1 tsp. |
| Nutmeg | 1/4 tsp. |
| Cinnamon | 2 tsp. |
| Nuts | 1/2 cup chopped: walnuts, pecans or almonds |
| Apples | 3 to 4 cup diced cooking apples |

PROCEDURE:

1. Beat together the two sugars, oil and eggs.
2. Mix the dry ingredients together.
3. Fold the flour mixture into the sugar mixture.
4. Add the apples and optional nuts.
5. Prepare and 13 x 9" pan with butter or cooking oil or parchment paper.
6. Bake 350 degrees for 35 minutes.

For extra treat, serve with a caramel sauce and for a double extra treat, add some dark rum to the caramel.

# LEMON YOGURT CAKE

This is a light and low fat cake that I have altered often, adding different flavors, but is really lovely just as is. This recipe is for a 9" pan but I double the recipe and bake it in a tube pan. Note the contrast of this recipe with the rich recipes of the 60's and 70's.

| | |
|---|---|
| Flour | 1 2/3 cups |
| Baking powder | 1 tsp. |
| Baking soda | 1 tsp. |
| Oil | 1/2 cup (I use canola) |
| Sugar | 3/4 cup |
| Vanilla extract | 1 tsp. |
| Egg whites | 3 |
| Plain yogurt | 1 cup (I use fat free) |
| Lemon juice | 1/4 cup |
| Sugar | 1/4 cup |

PROCEDURE:

1. Sift the flour, powder and soda together.
2. Beat together the oil, sugar, vanilla and eggs.
3. Mix at low speed the flour mixture alternately with the yogurt and the oil sugar mixture. 4. Turn into prepared pan (9" if you do not double the recipe).
5. Bake 350 degrees for 45 minutes or until cake tests done.
6. Mix lemon juice and 1/4 cup sugar and spoon over the hot cake.

Option: I often would make a mixture of brown sugar, ground nuts and oatmeal and put it on top of the cake, making it more like a coffee cake.

# TWO THANKSGIVING MENUS FROM THE 80's

Thanksgiving in the new kitchen...the dessert buffet.

**1981:** I do not know how many people but clearly it was vegetarians, meat eaters and children

**Appetizers:**
Spinach and cheese turnovers
Stuffed mushrooms
Spiced cheese pinwheels
Raw vegetables
Cheese and cracker tray
Assorted nuts

**Dinner:**
Roast turkey with bread stuffing
Cornbread stuffing and dried fruit (vegetarian)
Giblet gravy
Timbale of corn
Sweet peas
Mashed potatoes
Greens beans and red peppers
Lentil, bean and rice casserole
Spiced root vegetable platter (yams, turnips, squash) with chestnut ginger sauce
Boiled onions with leeks

Cranberries, apple sauce
Pear/pecan bread

**Dessert:**
Pecan pie
Apple crisp
Pumpkin pie
Krispie Squares (I am sure this is my sister's contribution…her famous Rice Krispies)
Brownies
Whipped cream
Cheese and fresh fruit

**1987**

**Appetizers:**
Cranberry punch
Cider
Wine
Crudities and dip
Cheese platter

**Dinner:**
Turkey
Gravy
Apple bread stuffing
Potato pancakes
Yams with ginger and orange
Braised carrots
Onions with almonds
Butternut squash
Parsnips and celeriac
Steamed green beans
Apple sauce, cranberries, olives
Corn muffins
Bran muffins (Now that is strange. What was I thinking?)

**Dessert:**
Apple pie
Pecan pie
Pumpkin pie
Chocolate cake
Whipped cream
Fresh fruit

## GREENSBORO, NORTH CAROLINA
## and FLOYD, VIRGINIA 1996-2000

Buying a house in North Carolina after spending much of our lives in New England was not as difficult as we thought. We found a gem that had been left vacant for two years and untouched for perhaps forty. Because of heat and humidity and the house unattended, it was moldy and in need of everything. This gave us an opportunity to buy it at a good price with money left over to remodel. The task was going to take six months, so we moved ourselves to a hospital provided apartment used most often for nursing students.

When counting kitchens, I didn't count this apartment because it really didn't have a kitchen, just a hot plate and a microwave. It is amazing what you can make with one burner. We actually did have guests for dinner. No baking. I have been trying to remember what I was cooking only having one burner and a microwave. I guess I could have boiled the water for pasta on the burner and microwaved a sauce. That sounds pretty bad. Maybe I made my favorite ketchup sauce! Joe would have hated that! Seriously, I am guessing it must have been a one-pot stew or a big cold seafood salad. All these are guesses but what I do remember is four of us sitting at the table in the kitchen and everyone really surprised that we actually had a dinner. We also had some overnight guests. Breakfast would have been easy and so would lunch, and then out to dinner. There were many choices of wonderful restaurants not far from our temporary home.

I wanted my new kitchen to be just like the one I left in Massachusetts, but space and budget meant some compromises. It was smaller, less dramatic and by far my favorite. I loved that kitchen, the white cabinets, some with glass doors, a softer granite color, and cozier. What was missing was a connection to outside, but that was available through the dining room. This large open space had enormous French doors that opened to an expansive deck that looked out over gardens that we spent hours in planning and executing. We brought the casual New England perennial flower garden to the formal landscaped South. Everything in North Carolina felt formal to us and our home was always a surprise to our new friends. White wicker with yellows and blues were a strong contrast to the formal interiors of most of our neighbors. Our whole style of entertaining was a puzzle to them and so were our politics.

Donald Duck Cola advertising poster made just before WWII.

Because of the war, the cola was never made. Sugar was too expensive. This poster was given to Joe by a patient in Salem. He was a collector and told us that, besides himself, the only other known owner of Donald Duck posters was Jerry Falwell. We owned this large one and a smaller one. Now they hang in our children's homes.

Pool and gardens. View from the deck off of the dining room.

Politics has often been my yardstick in making judgments. I grew up in the liberal suburbs of New York. We raised our children in the social consciousness of the 70's and 80's suburbs of Boston. In North Carolina, you never knew who was what because everyone was so polite until you heard the election results. When I say everyone was polite, I need to amend that. I had two conversations that were funny at the time but did give me pause to be concerned about where I was living. The first was at a Christmas Gala that the hospital gave every year for high-ranking administrators, the board of directors and important contributors. We were new and seated next to a gentleman with the thickest drawl I had heard in Greensboro. It was more than "yuall" and "bless your heart." This was as heavy as tar. When he heard I was from Massachusetts, he turned to face me, put his arm around my shoulder (yuck) and said:

" Now honey you didn't vote for Kennedy did you?"

Without missing a beat I said,

"You didn't vote for Jesse did you?"

He sat with his mouth opened, his arm moved off my shoulder and that was the last my dinner companion said to me. Oh, well you can't charm them all.
He knew that I was referring to Jesse Helms and was horrified that not only did I vote for Kennedy but was not a fan of a North Carolina's favorite, Jessie Helms.

The second encounter was a neighbor. Now let me say first off I really liked her and still have wonderful memories of our friendship. Her probing questions of me at our first meeting were never intended to be mean, she was just curious. I was candid and answered all her inquiries. After a few hours and many glasses of sweet ice tea (which should be considered a crime), she looked at me and said:

"So let me get this straight. You work full time, you're a Yankee, you're a Democrat and you're a vegetarian. Honey, you are not going to make it here!"

Being Jewish didn't seem to be the problem; it was all that other stuff. She was right that I didn't fit in, but it was not for any of the reasons she thought. I met Democrats and women who worked. No, the major problem was money. We were living in a neighborhood of wealth beyond our means and experience. Most of our neighbors' wealth came from textiles (which explains the tolerance of Jews since that was an industry started by the Jewish Cone brothers). Their social lives were expensive. I have never known a community to be as generous as Greensboro. Everything was about charity. All the balls and all the dinner parties were for charity. So they were buying expensive clothes, renting rooms at "the club," and hiring caterers to raise money for the needy. Unfortunately, the cost for attending these events was well beyond our budget. We gave to as many of these charities as we could, but never enough to get invited to a ball.

Over the five years in Greensboro, I spent many hours with my neighbors. Their views seemed to come from long traditions and the good fortune of wealth. I wonder now why I kept so much of myself private from this group and realize that it was for much the same reason I avoided conflict when teaching school in Marshfield. I think of myself as outspoken, even opinionated, but there are times and places where I don't trust enough to be real. I wanted my neighbors to like me. I wanted to fit in. I did not want them to view me odder than they already did (I could not hide the Yankee, working woman aspect of my life). Fortunately, I had some other friends who knew more about who I was so; I was not always walking on eggshells. But in the neighborhood, at Rotary and at work I was, most of the time, a chameleon.

Through my work at a private school for children with learning disabilities I was a member of the Rotary, which was about two hundred men and a dozen women. I watched everyone giving and supporting everyone else's charities and speaking with great passion about their own causes. It was amazing. I was always well behaved and respected. I had to be. It wasn't just the gender minority, the lack of wealth and a very minor professional standing; it was also that I was notably the shortest person in the room!

Not all my work-related experiences were positive and one episode changed my work life. The school for which I worked was very prestigious private school for students with learning disabilities. I was the director of admissions and supervised the school counselor. When I arrived at the school, most of the students were white males from families that could afford the tuition. We did have some scholarships, but they were limited. During my four years there, I brought in students from the local Jewish Day School and students of color. The school was starting to look different. The first year we had Jewish students (three families), the Parents' Open House was scheduled on the first night of a sacred Jewish Holiday. The three new families, who were looking forward to being involved in their student's new school, were not able to attend. The families called me in the hopes that the next year when the school planned the calendar that the most scared holiday of the Jewish faith would be considered. When I went to the next board meeting, I presented this request. One male board member, who was also the father of a student and the husband of a teacher, leaned back in his chair, put his hands behind his head and said:

"So if I belonged to the Church of Marijuana and I said next Tuesday is National Smoke Day, would we have to work around that too?"

I asked him if he was equating the Jewish faith with this Church of Marijuana that he just invented and he said: "What's the difference?"

No one else said anything.

I kept my cool and stayed through the rest of the meeting, but the next day I sent a letter to the board and said we needed to meet and I needed an apology. There were a few meetings and some said they understood how I felt, but no one felt an apology was due nor did they see any reason to change their calendar to meet the needs of three families. I resigned. I never wore my faith on my sleeve or anywhere else, but I felt this was unjust and demonstrated a not so subtle prejudice. I did not feel like fighting windmills.

The director and a few board members tried to undo the damage, but it was too late. I never told any of the staff the truth. I just said I was opening up a private practice. I am sure they all knew and there was lots of gossip.

My last year in Greensboro, I struggled trying to get a private practice going. I had a few clients and a lovely office. The most important part was my personal feelings of pride in what I did and lots and lots of support from the Jewish community. The word spread fast from one friend to another and to the local Rabbi.

The generosity of our neighbors to charity was contagious. Joe and I volunteered at a homeless shelter and I served on two boards for organizations that dealt with issues of children in need. We slowly met people who shared our values and started to have a good sense of community. One of my volunteering situations brought me to another standoff and I was the offender. But with hard work, something good really great came of it. I met with a large group of mother's weekly dealing with issues of parenting. It was a bit too large a group to have intimate conversations, but we did try to make a large circle with our chairs and have honest dialogues. I was the facilitator, not the teacher. One day the conversation turned to spanking. Someone asked me what I thought. I told my favorite true story.

When Jon was a toddler in Minneapolis, he had a play date. The mom and her son were at our apartment. Her son hit mine. The mother then hit her son and said "we don't hit." If it weren't so sad, it would be funny. So I used this story of an example of how I think spanking gives kids the wrong message. Did I mention that almost all the mothers in the group were African American? Now that bit of information is important. One parent called me a racist. She went on to explain (a well educated women with a professional job) that spanking is part of her culture and religion.

"You had no right to sit in judgment of our culture!"

The room got loud with many opinions. I was quiet and sorry I had caused this controversy and felt trapped, but as the argument grew, I held my ground. I tried to steer the conversation to a more philosophical view of culture and "what is racism?" I shared that there are many things in my personal "tribe" that I was not proud of and yet I resent when people use those behaviors as negative stereotypes. I shared that just because I felt that spanking had many negative results, it did not mean that I was judging African American parenting. Some parents did not believe me when I told them I never thought of spanking as part of their tradition or culture. I tried hard not to back down from my point of view, but gave them lots of opportunity to yell at me. Not everyone was angry and some, in fact, agreed with me, but not this one mother. She was mad and was waiting for an apology. The best she could get was that I was sorry I offended her, but I stood firm on my beliefs just like she was firm in hers. (Hmm, sounds like I was now on the other side of the table. Did that board member who I felt insulted me feel as I did now with this angry mother?)

After the meeting, I went up to the mother and asked if we could talk some more. She was in a hurry, but said she would call me.

We had at least five very long telephone conversations, and it became quite clear that she was devoted in her faith and was determined to convert me. After close to five hours of getting to know one another, she said:

"I just don't get it. You are not a believer but still seem to be a good person."

We both accomplished what we wanted. I understood her beliefs and was working hard to respect them, and she learned that we can walk a different path and still be human. It ended better than I hoped, neither of us changing our core beliefs but knowing that good people can have different opinions. I wonder what her kids are like and whether mine would <u>have benefitted from a kick in the pants.</u>

Our life in Greensboro was full and interesting, but we felt a strong pull to have some escape. We bought a beautiful piece of land in Floyd, Virginia. We were poking around the towns that were two hours or less from Greensboro in the foothills near the Blue ridge Parkway. We just had such a strong pull to get back to the mountains, missing Maine. We fell in love with Floyd not knowing much about it except for a beautiful, and within our budget, piece of property. It was on a river filled with healthy trees and a covered picnic pavilion. We took that picnic pavilion, enclosed it with a few walls and French doors, and added a screened porch and a small bathroom. We had one large room with six French doors and two tiny bedrooms. The kitchen ran along one wall. The cabinets were stock from a home supply chain and the counters were homemade. (Joe knew how to do it properly now). The refrigerator was small and the stove small, but efficiently heated by propane.

Picnic Pavilion before its conversion.

Kitchen/living room

Jazz on our porch

Joe's interpretation

This idyllic spot that we thought was a small gem turned out to be a diamond. Floyd was a destination for artists looking for rural life not far from an academic center (Virginia Tech was less than an hour away). We, by some quirk of good luck, were welcomed as members of a small intimate group of artists living along the river and in the hills of Floyd. They were mostly potters but all the arts were represented. They had been together since their early adult years when most of them left the Northeast or Midwest. They must have seen in us people who had chosen a different path, but were hungry to immerse themselves into their lifestyle. We fawned over their art and crafts, and soaked up as much information as they could share. We hiked together, we played in the river, but mostly we cooked, ate, and drank wine and laughed together. We also shared a love of jazz. We organized a jazz group where we would get together once a month for live music and potluck suppers. The idea caught on and, since the Virginia Hills were "alive with music," it was easy to find a musician who would jam for very little money. They would join us for dinner and often became part of the group. The idea caught on, and more and more people wanted to join. Since most of our homes were small, we had to limit our winter numbers, but in the summer we grew and grew. Mostly the music was wonderful but for me even more than the music was the joy I got looking around the room and seeing all the really cool people who were now part of my life. I loved every weekend in Floyd! I loved the simple pleasures of being with people whose lives we envied. We now know that living off of your art is not easy but at that time we had a romantic image of their lives.

For five years, Floyd, Virginia was a true home and community. It is also why, after we left North Carolina, we tried to make our lives mirror their lives—working at being artists. Check out the website "16hands.com" to learn about this community of artists.

Floyd, Virginia was our weekend life but our real life had to be Greensboro. We had a wonderful house, perhaps our best. We had a lap pool, our view was a golf course and neighbors who had big beautiful homes and saw the world through a special lens. Our views were challenged, but it gave us many opportunities to reassess and redefine who we were and what we wanted. If we had stayed in New England, in our comfort zone, there is so much we would never have learned. We even tried out really being Jewish and joined a Temple. It was there that we met many friends and had a social relationship with the Rabbi and his wife. He was not horrified that we had never belonged to a Temple before.

Although our work, politics and social lives were interesting and important, our life still centered in the kitchen. All thoughts of food and Greensboro start with our first Thanksgiving. Jonathan was living in San Francisco and Wendy in Cambridge, two of our favorite cities. That first year, they brought guests. Jon brought Felicia and Wendy brought Matthew. Since then Felicia and Matthew have become important members of our family.

Wendy and Matthew, both vegetarians, meant the table was laden with a wide variety of vegetables and grains. Jon and Felicia were looking forward to traditional fare, so a large turkey and stuffing were happily included. Years later, I learned that I knocked everyone's socks off with the dessert buffet (we had invited friends to join us for dessert). But what I most remember was the look on Felicia's face when she saw me throw away all the turkey bones. " No soup?" Oops. She grew up not wasting any part of the fowl. The next year, her parents joined us for Thanksgiving and her mother, Flo, made a wonderful soup.

**Recipes from the 1990's**

In the 1990's, with our two children leaving home and starting independent lives, our days as vegetarians started to wane and we began to feel restless.

It wasn't until 1996 that we moved to North Carolina, but we started thinking about a change for many years before. We seem to be entertaining less often and making dishes that were less complex. We maintained the concept of thinking about what we ate, but moved away from the strict vegetarian diet.

It was a high carb time for us. Pasta found its way into much of our daily living. Most of those dishes had no recipes and were mostly what was available with tomatoes and olive oil. When looking through my notebooks I saw that I made "cakes." These cakes were made with vegetables and fish and served for a light meal or appetizer. It is also a great way to use leftovers. We would rarely have a dinner that did not start with a salad, but I have included very few salad recipes. Delicious greens, some vegetables, and a lemon and olive oil dressing was our standard. In this chapter, you will see a few salads because I think they go well with the savory cakes.

As the decade drew to a close, fish became more and more important and I learned that fresh fish requires little preparation and rarely a recipe. All you need is a hot grill, lemon, olive oil and a few fresh herbs. So, although there are few fish recipes that is what we were eating in the 90's and into the next century. Dessert: fruit and sorbet and homemade cookies, fruit pies and low fat chocolate cake.

# EIGHT SAVORY CAKES

Vegetable, fish and potato "cakes" make wonderful side dishes and appetizers, they can be served with a salad or part of a brunch. Once you get the concept, the combinations of ingredients are endless. These are just a few of ones I have made.

Most of these recipes are two steps. Mix the ingredients together and then either bake or cook in a heavy skillet. Either cooking method will work. Do not deep fat fry any of them. They are meant to be light and not greasy.

## *CORN FRITTERS:
Mix the following together:
1 1/2 cup flour
2 tsp. baking powder
1/4 tsp. salt
1/2 cup milk (skim is fine)
2 egg whites
1 cup corn kernels
1/2 cup diced red sweet pepper
black pepper
 Season with any combination of the following:
  cumin, oregano, parsley and cilantro

Form into cakes and place on a baking sheet lined with parchment and brushed with olive oil. Bake about 10 minutes on each side.
OR… You can brown the cakes in a heavy skillet. Do not deep fry.
*Substitute black beans for the corn for black bean fritters

## CORN CAKES FOR CAVIAR OR SMOKED SALMON:
 Mix the following together
  1 1/2 cups corn kernels, roughly chopped
  1/2 cup milk
  1/3 cup cornmeal
  4 Tbsp. butter, melted
  3 eggs
  1/2 tsp. salt
  1/2 tsp. black pepper
  1/4 cup chopped chives

Follow the preparation of baking on a prepared pan or cook in a skillet until they are golden brown.
Serve with sour cream and caviar or smoked salmon and cream cheese.

**SWEET POTATO PANCAKES:**
Mix together:
2 grated yams
1 grated russet potatoes
1/2 cup flour
2 egg whites
salt and pepper

Form into cakes and brown in oven or in a heavy skillet. Serve with a tomato salsa for a unique taste combination.

**MUSHROOM CAKES:**
Oven 350 degrees
Heat: 1Tbsp. oil in heavy skillet
Sauté: 1 lb. wild mushrooms, chopped
1/2 medium onion, finely chopped
*Transfer cooked mushrooms and onions to a bowl*
Peel and grate: 1 tart apple and stir into mushroom mixture
Peel and slice very thin: 1 lb. Yukon gold potatoes.
Slice: 1/2 medium onion and add to potato slices. Salt and pepper
Heat 2 Tbsp. olive oil in heavy ovenproof skillet
Assemble:
1/3 of potato and onion slices in 1 layer bottom of skillet top with 1/2 mushroom mixture, spreading evenly
Repeat layering with potatoes, mushrooms and top with potatoes.
Put skillet in oven and bake for 20 minutes
Invert on a round platter or pizza pan. Slide the cake back into the skillet so the bottom is now on top.
Press layers together with a spatula.
Bake until crusty 8 to 10 minutes.

**VEGETABLE CAKES:**

Dice: 1cup celery
       1cup carrots
       1cup sweet onion
Sauté until soft
Add; 1cup fresh peas
       1cup fresh chopped spinach
       1cup diced and seeded tomato
Cook enough to get rid of any liquid. Do not overcook.
Season with chopped basil, parsley, thyme, salt and pepper.
Cook: 1 lb. potatoes until soft, then mash.
Whisk: 4 large egg whites
Stir: egg whites into the mashed potatoes until smooth.
Add: vegetables. Taste for flavor.
Make cakes.
Cover top and bottom of each cake in breadcrumbs.
Sauté cakes until brown.
Can be reheated at serving time.


**SHRIMP CAKES:**

Blend together in a food processor:
       6 oz. sea scallops
       1/2 cup Japanese bread crumbs (Panko)
       2 egg whites
       2 Tbsp. yogurt (any dairy, even cream, works)
       salt and pepper
Blend until smooth.
Add:
       6 oz. shrimp ( peeled and deveined)
       1/3cup cilantro, chopped
       2 Tbsp. chives, chopped
       2Tbsp. parsley, chopped
       1 cup panko (more if needed)
Chill 1 hour or overnight.
Pan fry cakes until golden, about 4 minutes per side.

## SALMON/SHRIMP CAKES:

Steam: 1lb. potatoes that have been peeled and diced
Mash: potatoes*
Steam: 6 oz. firm flesh fish, about 10 minutes. Flake the cooked fish
Add: fish to the potatoes
Mix:
    ¼ lb. bay shrimp, chopped
    2 oz. smoked salmon, chop
    1/2 cup green onions
    1/4 cup fresh dill, chopped
    2 tsp. grated lemon peel

Season with salt and pepper.
Shape fish into balls and then flatten into 1/2' thick cakes.
Put 2 cups of breadcrumbs in a shallow bowl. Coat each cake with the crumbs. Brown in heavy skillet coated with about 3 Tbsp. of oil.

* I do not always use potatoes. A bit of panko breadcrumbs and a few egg whites (or whole eggs) hold the cakes together. If this is a side dish or appetizer, it is less filling without the potatoes.


## SALMON CORN CAKES:

Heat: 4 tsp. olive oil in a skillet
Add: 2 small leeks, trimmed and finely chopped
1 1/2 cup shitake mushrooms, chopped Cook and
   then put in a bowl.
Add: 12 oz. cooked salmon, coarsely chopped
2 eggs, beaten
    1/4 cup chopped chives
    1/4 cup cornmeal
    salt and pepper

Form into 12 cakes.
Heat a heavy skillet and lightly coat with oil.
Coat each cake with cornmeal. 1/4 cup in a shallow bowl should be enough to cover 12 cakes.

Cook about 2 minutes on each side, until brown. They can be reheated.

## SALADS AND SAUCES THAT GO WELL WITH SAVORY CAKES

**CORN SALAD:**

Mix together:
- 1 cup corn
- 1 cup seeded, diced cucumber
- 1 cup red onion. Diced
- 1 cup seeded diced tomato
- 1 Tbsp. lemon juice
- 1 Tsp. grated ginger
- 1 jalapeno pepper minced
- 1 Tbsp. cilantro, chopped
- Cayenne pepper (optional)

**GINGER COLE SLAW:**

Combine:
- 1 head of green cabbage, shredded
- 1 cup red cabbage, shredded
- 1 cup peeled carrots, shredded
- 1/2 cup sweet red pepper, chopped
- 1/2 cup onion, chopped (optional)

Whisk together:
- 1/2 cup olive oil
- 1/2 cup sugar
- 1/2 cup white balsamic vinegar
- 1 tsp. dry mustard
- 1/4 tsp. ground gin

**CARROT SALAD:**

Cook together:
- 1 lb. carrots, peeled and halved
- 1/2 cup water
- 1/4 tsp. coriander seeds
- 1/4 tsp. crushed dried red pepper

Cook until the carrots are tender but still crisp.

Uncover pot and cook until the water evaporates, about 1 minute. Put in serving bowl and cool.

Mix together:
- 1 1/2 tsp. ground cumin
- 2 Tbsp. lemon juice
- 1 Tbsp. olive oil

Add to carrots:
- 1/3 cup chopped red onion
- 1/3 cup chopped cilantro
- 1/3 cup Kalamata olives, chopped

**ROOT VEGETABLE SLAW:**

Mix together:
- 1/2 cup celery root, julienned
- 1/2 cup carrots, julienned
- 1/2 cup parsnips, julienned

1 Tbsp. apple cider vinegar, or an herbed flavored balsamic vinegar
1 Tbsp. chopped parsley
  salt and pepper
Optional: a splash of olive oil


**ZUCCHINI AND FENNEL SLAW:**

Mix together:

1 medium zucchini, grated
1/2 fennel bulb, thinly sliced
2 Tbsp. olive oil
3 1 Tbsp. lemon juice
4 handfuls chopped mint
 salt and pepper


**BEET, CARROT AND FENNEL SALAD:**

Beets: three red beets. Peel and cut into quarters. I like to roast them but they can be steamed. Do not boil.
Carrots: 4 peeled and sliced. Roast or steam.
Fennel: 1 bulb, sliced. Roast or sauté.
Roasting suggestion: cover large baking sheet with parchment paper and olive oil. You can roast all the vegetables together, but their cooking time will be different. The beets take about 40 minutes and then fennel about 15 minutes but you should check them often to see if they are done to the tenderness you prefer. Remove the cooked vegetables to a bowl.

When all the vegetables are cooked and cooled, add a simple vinaigrette.
I like olive oil, lemon juice, a splash of vinegar and a tsp. of honey mustard with these vegetables. Your flavors should be consistent with the other dishes.

**RED PEPPER COULIS:**

Cook in a large skillet:
- ½ lb. red peppers, cored, seeded and diced
- 1 tomato, seeded and diced
- 1/2 large onion, diced
- 1 3/4 cup tomato juice
- 1/4 cup chopped basil
- 1/8 tsp. thyme

Cook and then blend to a sauce.


**CUCUMBER MINT SAUCE:**

Process:
- 1/4 cup fresh mint leaves
- 1/2 jalapeno pepper, seeded and chopped

Add: 1 cucumber, peeled, seeded and process until finely chopped

Stir into the cucumber mixture:
- 8 oz. nonfat plain yogurt
- 1 scallion, thinly sliced
- salt

Chill.

# SALMON/EGGPLANT SUMMER DINNER PARTY

Appetizer platter:
> Sundried tomatoes, assorted olives, goat cheese, artichoke hearts and roasted red peppers. Bread and crackers.

Soup:

### Cold Green Pea and Mint
No exact recipe. The ingredients are frozen peas and large handful of flavorful but soft lettuce, lightly cooked onion and chicken broth. Cook the peas, onions and lettuce in the broth. Puree, Add salt and pepper and lots of mint. Serve with yogurt or sour cream.

Dinner:

### Salmon and Eggplant Stack
**Eggplant:** Cut into thick slices. Rub each slice with olive oil and rub with a garlic clove, salt and pepper. Grill.

**Salmon:** Marinate in lime juice, black pepper and olive oil. Grill.

**Polenta:** Cook the polenta adding parsley, oregano, salt and pepper. Put the cooked polenta on a cookie sheet or 9x13 pan and cool. Cut into rectangles. Grill (less than a minute on each side).

**Black Beans:** Cook, puree into a thick paste.

**Fire Roasted Tomato Salsa:** buy your favorite. (Trader Joe's is good) Assemble on each plate:

1 stack:
1 eggplant slice
2 Tbsp. black bean spread
    Salmon
    Salsa
2 triangles of polenta sprinkled with cheese
  4 slices of avocado and a lime wedge
  Spoonful of sour cream
  Cilantro sprinkled over everything

Dessert:
### Trio of sorbet:
    Mango/ginger
    Strawberry with almond syrup
    Peach with vanilla syrup

# WINTER CHICKEN STEW

This is a recipe that I have made so many times with what was handy. As with most stews. it is a little bit of this and a little bit of that. I have no amounts since I have never really made it the same way twice. I like these seasonings in the winter but you will have to do it by taste.

Boneless, skinless chicken breast cut in cubes
Diced parsnips
Diced carrots
Diced fingerling potatoes:
Sliced onion
Diced turnip
Diced apples
Assorted wild mushrooms: sliced (not too many or could overpower flavor but enough to add richness)
Firm root vegetables
Chickpeas
Seasonings:( to taste)
salt and pepper,
cayenne pepper
coriander
cardamom
cumin
cinnamon
curry (sparingly)
thyme and parsley
chicken or vegetable stock (at least 5 cups)

PROCEDURE:

1. Large pot, saute onions until soft
2. Add mushrooms. Add rest of vegetables and quickly saute for a few seconds
3. Add chicken or vegetable stock. Enough to cook vegetables
4. In large fry pan place half of all seasoing and coat pan with olive oil
5. Saute chicken pieces until cooked
6. Add chicken to vegetables
7. In a small saucepan add 1 1/2 cup of stock, 2 Tbsp. of flour that has been made into a paste with butter cook until it is like light cream. Pour sauce over stew
8. Put stew in casserole and bake until hot
9. Optional: cover the top with phyllo pastry. Bake until the crust is brown.

# DINNER PARTY MENU IN GREENSBORO, NORTH CAROLINA

This was a dinner and sleepover party. Some of our friends from Floyd, Virginia came for the weekend and slept at our house. We were all in our jeans, hanging out, cooking, eating and drinking wine. We really miss the easy entertaining and companionship we had the five years in the South.

Appetizer:

**Wild Mushroom and Goat Cheese Tart**
Tart pastry is not that different from pie crust, but usually has an egg so it is more like a cookie dough. The assorted mushrooms are sautéd with chopped shallots, thyme, salt and pepper. Partially cook the tart shell so it is slightly firm. This can be done in advance. Mix a generous amount of goat cheese with the mushrooms and bake in the tart shell. You can add egg to make it more custard-like, but I like it just the cheese, mushrooms and shallots.

**Caponata**
Recipe is included in the 1980's chapter

Dinner:
> **Salad:** greens, lentils, asparagus, fennel and parmesan cheese
>
> Each plate is set up with the contrast of colors and is very attractive and tasty with an oil an vinegar dressing.

**Bouillabaisse\*:** sea bass, scallops, squid and shrimp

Julia Child's Mastering the Art of French Cooking pg. 52
Julia Child's The French Chief Cookbook pg. 36

The bouillabaisse recipe is Julia Child's and is my favorite company dish when I know my guests like seafood. It can be made with any available fish, but I think the more shells, the more fun to eat. I do use bottled clam broth, as she recommends, to the alternative of making your own fish stock. I love the taste and the ease of preparation. Fennel and orange peel cannot be eliminated.

Dessert:
> **Poached pears en croute with caramel sauce**
>
> **Apricots and crystalized ginger dipped in chocolate**

The pears are not very complicated to make. Core and peel the bottom third of each pear. Roll each in a mixture of cinnamon and sugar. Make a butter pastry dough or use a frozen commercial one.
Cut the pastry in squares.
Place the center of the square on top of the pear stem, letting the stem poke a hole so it sticks up. Encase the pear in the pastry, tucking the four corners in the hole in the bottom of the pear. Bake 350 degrees until the crust is golden and the pear juices start to run out.

# INDIAN-INSPIRED DINNER PARTY

Appetizer:

**Crudities with yogurt, cheese and spicy tomato chutney**

Dinner:

**Chicken with Yogurt**

Chicken cut into pieces marinated in yogurt, salt and pepper.
Combine and process until smooth:
> 1 onion, 3 cloves of garlic, 1/4 cup fresh ginger, 1 tsp. chili, 1 tsp. coriander,
> 1 tsp. cardamom, 1/2 tsp. cloves, 1/8 tsp. turmeric Cook the spices in butter and
> oil for 5 minutes.

Cook the chicken in a large skillet with yogurt, the cooked spices and enough broth to cover. Cover the pan. Just before serving add a handful of chopped cilantro.

**Dal with Tomatoes**

1 cup red lentils. Cook 2 Tbsp. ginger, 1 Tbsp. garlic and 1 onion, slivered, in oil and butter for 10 minutes. Add 2 tsp. cumin, 1/8 tsp. cloves, 1/8 tsp. turmeric.
Add the lentils and 4 cups broth. Boil. Reduce the heat and simmer uncovered. Add 4 seeded and diced plum tomatoes, salt, pepper and parsley.

**Marigold Rice**

Put 1 cinnamon stick, 5 cloves and cardamom in cheesecloth. Using a pot or rice cooker, place 8 cups of broth or water, 3 cups of rice, 1 cup diced carrots, 1 Tbsp. turmeric and the spices in the cheesecloth.
Cook until rice is done and remove the spices in the cheesecloth.

**Raita**

Add to 2 cup of yogurt: 1 1/2 tsp. ginger, 1/2 tsp. cumin, 2 plum tomatoes seeded and diced and 2 cucumbers, seeded and diced
Just before serving, add a large handful of chopped fresh mint.

**Peas, Potato and Cauliflower**

Cut the vegetables in small pieces and steam. Season with commercial Garam Marsala and a dash of molasses.

**Assorted chutneys**

## LOW FAT CHOCOLATE CAKE

This cake, although low fat, is surprisingly good. If you do not want the fat from the butter cream frosting, eliminate it. The cake can stand on its own, or use a wonderful jam as a glaze. Apricot is very nice. Just heat the jam and spread it on the cake. For extra fruit flavor, add chopped dried apricots on top of the glaze.

Dry ingredients:

2 1/4 cup flour
1 1/2 cup sugar
1 1/2 tsp. baking soda
3/4 tsp. salt
4 1/2 Tbsp. cocoa

Place the dry ingredients in a bowl. Mix and make a well and add:

1 Tbsp. white vinegar
1 1/2 tsp. vanilla
1 1/2 cup water
1/2 cup oil

Blend well with a wire whisk. Bake in a loaf pan or a spring form or angel food cake pan.

350 degrees for about 45 minutes (depending on pan).

When the cake cools, cut it in half. Spread raspberry (or any other flavor) jam between the layers.

A chocolate butter cream for the top and sides.

Freezes well.

## CHOCOLATE SPICED COOKIES

| | |
|---|---|
| Almonds | 1 1/2 cup |
| Sugar | 1 cup |
| Unsweetened cocoa | 1/4 cup |
| Cinnamon | 1 1/2 tsp. |
| Cloves, ground | 1/2 tsp. |
| Bittersweet chocolate | 4 oz. finely chopped |
| Egg whites | 2 |
| Almond extract | 1/4 tsp. |

PROCEDURE:

1. Use a food processor and pulse: almonds, sugar, cocoa, cinnamon and cloves, until finally finely ground.
2. Add 2 oz. of chocolate and pulse until fine ground.
3. Add egg whites and almond extract and pulse until the dough holds together.
4. Place dough on a 16" piece of plastic wrap. Wrap the dough and shape into a 10 x 2" log.
5. Chill in the freezer for 2 hours or overnight.
6. Preheat the oven 300 degrees.
7. Line 3 baking sheets with parchment paper.
8. Remove the dough from the freezer. Cut 1/8" slices.
9. Place the cookies 1" apart on cookie sheets
10. Bake each sheet one at a time on the middle shelf of the oven.
11. Bake 10 to 12 minutes until they are set but still soft.
12. Melt remaining 2 oz. of chocolate and drizzle over the cookies.
13. Let the cookies harden. They freeze well but stay at room temperature for 5 days.

# THREE THANKSGIVING MENUS FROM THE 90's

**1995**
**Appetizer**: Spiced shrimp
**Dinner**:
Roasted turkey breast
Herb stuffing
"Exotic" mushroom gravy (I am guessing I was using wild mushrooms)
Multigrain Risotto
Mashed potatoes
Spinach pie
Sweet potato puree
Brussels sprouts with garlic, lemon and sesame
Carrots with ginger and maple syrup
Onions and parsnips with sherry
Cranberries and applesauce
Gingerbread
**Dessert**: (I would sometimes invite people who had their own dinners to come for dessert.)
Apple pie
Pecan pie
Peach/cherry pie
Pumpkin pie
Chocolate torete
Pumpkin flan
Chocolate charlotte
Baked Pineapple

## 1996

**Appetizers:**
(None noted. I am sure there were at least some crudities.)

**Dinner:**
Turkey
Tofu vegetable walnut loaf
Wild mushroom vegetarian gravy
Herb and chestnut stuffing
Brussels sprouts with sun-dried tomatoes
Ginger honey glazed carrots
Green beans with roasted onion
Mashed potatoes with garlic
Yam puree in squash cups
Apple sauce and cranberry sauce
Corn muffins

**Dessert:**
Apple pie
Pumpkin pie
Pecan pie
Ginger cake
Cookies

## 1999

**Appetizer:**
(Again, I make no mention, but since our guests were there for the weekend, I am sure there was **a lot of snack food out.**)

**Dinner:**
Sage roasted turkey
Cornbread and wild rice stuffing
Wild mushroom Maderia gravy
Roasted chestnuts and caramelized baby onions
Sweet potatoes, candied ginger and oranges
Brussels sprouts with shallots and port
Applesauce
Cranberry/ginger sauce

**Dessert:**
Pumpkin pie
Apple pie with caramel sauce
Chocolate orange layer cake
Fruit
Cheese

## KIRKLAND, WASHINGTON 2000-2001

Five years gave us time to learn and appreciate the beauty of the South. It was also enough time for us to know that we could not stay in the South long-term. Home was still a search. The retreat in Virginia would have been a terrific place to live, but we still needed jobs and there was nothing there for us. It was time to look for another hospital that needed Joe's talents as a chief medical officer. Kirkland, Washington: a challenging job, a part of the country that we had not experienced made this offer hard to refuse. We sold the large four-bedroom, five-bathroom house with a lap pool and the dream kitchen. We sold the cabin in the mountains and moved to an expanded "A frame" and again tried not looking back.

We fell in love with this quirky little house with no dining room and a small living room, which only had room for one couch. The recently added upstairs master bedroom had panoramic views of Lake Washington, the Space Needle and, on rare sunny days, it looked as if Mt. Rainier was in our yard. We were able to make a charming dining room out of a hallway that connected the kitchen to a bedroom, which was now a den. It was perfect. The backyard was a small courtyard with a guest cottage, so we had no need for the spare bedroom. The kitchen was very small but somehow it worked for cooking. A rented storage unit handled our massive amount of kitchen stuff that we really didn't need.

Doesn't it sound perfect? It was for a few months, until we learned that our neighbors had a permit issued before we bought the house. The permit was to build a structure taller than our home that would house their motor home. When constructed, this was a three-story cement wall that blocked many of our views and sunlight. Our once wonderful master suite/family room was now just a big room. No views of the space needle and limited views of the lake, but it was the sun I missed. Now all the compromises we didn't mind (the lack of dining room, tiny living room and galley kitchen) became annoyances. Closets? We did not realize we had only one decent closet and it was in the master bathroom. Not a great place when you have two people trying to get showered and dressed to go to work. It was tight quarters.

Despite the loss of light and views, we still had much to make this new life positive. We lived one block from a wonderful ceramic studio and I had an opportunity to start my redefinition. Still working as a school counselor, but part time, I had the time, motivation and opportunity to learn to be a potter. Cooking was now on the" back burner." Simple, easy ingredients were ideal for our health, our small kitchen and our new lifestyle.

Living two blocks from the lake and downtown Kirkland, we had a new evening routine. Kirkland is the home of art galleries. We would take a long walk along the lakefront, stop at galleries and then end up at a steakhouse that had a beautiful bar and friendly bartenders. A glass of wine and a small salad and friendly conversation helped to transition from the day's activities. A steep hill walk back to our home and dinner seemed the perfect routine. Dinner could be soup, a vegetable and tofu stew, pasta or some fish on the grill. We met some nice people on these outings and also found that Joe and I talked to one another about our day more than when at home. It was like a date every night without the expense of eating out.

Kirkland was an ideal location to take public transportation into Seattle. We did it often and fell in love with the small town feel with the big city culture. (We would find this again in another city). The easy lifestyle was a perfect match for us. People entertained in their homes and spent most of their free time outdoors, never letting the constant light rain stop any plans. We also had easy access to explore Western Washington and Vancouver.

We joined a health club, I joined a book club, we met people who liked to cook and we did not have to pretend. We could be ourselves, share our views, and have interesting conversations and lots of fun. We were not odd, different or wacky, because everyone else was too! You could not tell the homeless from the Microsoft billionaires. They all dressed the same: scruffy shorts and tee shirts was the dress code. Even though there was great wealth, it just didn't show that much.

Seattle was a great match for us except, and this was important, for Joe's job. The hospital was in crisis and Joe made major positive changes, but he felt frustrated.

We were not planning on moving, but an interesting job in California became too tempting. We loved Seattle, but a move to California would bring us closer to Jon and Felicia and an easier plane trip for Wendy and Matthew. So we put the house on the market knowing the new buyers were not looking at the same house we bought. The market value reflected the loss of views. Not ones to spend too much time looking at what we had lost, we were ready for our next adventure. Less money in our pockets, but we packed up our house and the storage unit and moved everything to a smaller one-bedroom cottage and a bigger storage unit and were again looking forward to a new adventure.

Kirkland kitchen with a view of dining table in the hall. This is the last house that we used some of our treasured primitive pieces of furniture from New England. When we moved, we gave much of it away. I loved my wooden apples in the stoneware bowl. They, too, would no longer be seen.

## NEVADA CITY CALIFORNIA, 2001-2002

**NEVADA CITY, CALIFORNIA** 2001-2002 (picket fence and a gate you could swing on)

This little cottage was in a town in the foothills of northern California. It was once a gold mining town and now home to aging hippies, young wannabe hippies, people who wanted a simpler life and left the city, or the wonderful people whose families lived there for multiple generations.

This one-bedroom cottage was a stopping place for us while we built our "retirement" home 14 miles away in a more rural part of the county. We were building our first home and the plan was that it would be the last, but for the time being, we were living in the cutest little cottage. The kitchen needed attention but not the granite, hardwood floor kind. We knew we were going to sell it in about a year and did not want to invest more than the house would be worth. We went Formica and linoleum shopping. The white counters and white with bits of blue flooring and white cabinets made the room sparkle. Touches of blue, new appliances and the kitchen had a universal appeal. It certainly appealed to me. I loved the white and the blue accents just felt crisp and clean. The one bedroom and living room were painted and the basement became usable living space. They were all fun projects and not too expensive. There was an out building that was bigger than the house that became a pottery studio and woodworking shop. This was our first attempt at living like our Floyd friends. We put in our favorite French doors in the out building and had views of a lovely cluster of trees. The front of the house needed a white picket fence and gate and, once that was completed, we started to fall in love with our little house and wondered why we were moving. Our first grandson, Benjamin, was born while we lived in our cottage. Our finished basement gave our growing family a place to sleep when visiting.

While we lived in this cottage, we heard Joan Baez sing in a room small enough to feel her voice. That close. The vibrations went through our bodies. Quite a contrast to the last time we had heard her, in a large hall in Cambridge, Massachusetts. Some of the people in the audience in Nevada City actually were friends of hers. She was singing to people she knew and about issues she cared about. We had almost forgotten how powerful an experience it is to hear politics sung by a voice that had been with us through all our transitions. A few years later in Berkeley, I was standing behind her in line for the ladies room. We were both with our granddaughters at a small production of "The Nutcracker." I smiled at her but never told her how our lives have crossed so many times. She did smile at me…two grandmas with young granddaughters.

While we lived in our cottage, we met people who collected crystals, hung flags from Tibet, knew about Sufi dancing and had spiritual beliefs that mystified us. We welcomed these new people and their ideas and learned a lot, but in the end were not able to embrace it. We felt like tourists in a foreign land trying to assimilate but never able to learn the language. Little did we know that our next move would bring us to not only a "foreign land," but to ideologies we never could begin to understand no matter how hard we tried.

Me at my wheel            Joe building the fence

## PENN VALLEY, CALIFORNIA 2002-2004

While we lived in that fairytale cottage, we were building our "dream home" that we were going to live in the rest of our lives. We bought 46 acres of pastureland with western views of the Sutter Buttes and nothing but sky and hills in between. I designed the house, every bit of it: the good, the bad and the silly. A draftsperson converted my drawings so we could get permits but changed nothing. Joe was in transition from one hospital job to another and was able to take most of the year off. He worked on the construction crew. This was really going to be our home. (He designed and built the beautiful shutters.)

The design was strongly influenced by our little cabin in the Blue Ridge Mountains of Virginia. Lots of doors in every room all opening to the outdoors. The house was filled with light and views. The major space, and perhaps too large for cozy comfort, was the living room, dining room and kitchen, all open and pretty fabulous to look at. The master bedroom, the TV room and guest room were all just right for us, but too small for buyers when it came time to sell. There was a large walk-in pantry, laundry room that looked like a real room, and a screened in porch. But what really put this house over the top was the second structure. The second building was almost as large as the main house and was two stories. Downstairs: a potter's studio, a woodworking shop and a gallery. There was also a large storage area mostly for gardening equipment. Upstairs: an apartment for our kids when they came to visit. It was everything we hoped for until we met our neighbors. The first to greet us were the rattlesnakes. We had moved into their home turf and they were mad. They were everywhere and we were terrified. Even with all the land, they made it hard to garden. I was never comfortable with even looking at photos of snakes, let alone have them sharing my home. We heard about a "snake guy." He trapped snakes and brought them elsewhere. The elsewhere was never disclosed. He also attempted to educate us about snakes and worked at getting people more comfortable with their presence, keeping in mind that all our snakes were rattlesnakes and dangerous. We learned that the babies were the most dangerous. We hired him before we had moved in to help us deal and to try to remove as many as possible. One day, while we were getting our lesson and I was being encouraged to actually touch a snake he had in a cage, we saw our painter run out of the room he was painting. A snake was in the house! I was ready to go back to our little cottage and scrap this plan of a "dream" home. The snake guy was great and hung in there with my anxiety, and I did start to feel a bit better. We were told to get guinea hens because they kill the snakes. After we moved in, Joe built "homes" for our two- dozen hens. They would peck at the snakes and kill them. One morning, we discovered all our hens were either gone or had been left to die. Coyotes had attacked them. Nature untamed can be scary.

This looks like a very hungry snake waiting to eat a guinea hen in one bite!

When planting our fruit trees, vegetables and flowers in temperatures sometime 100 degrees, we wore long pants, heavy boots and heavy gloves. This was to protect us from the snakes. Besides the snakes and coyotes, there were mountain lions and the cute deer that liked to eat everything. We were learning how to live with these neighbors, not easily, but we were trying. What we did not learn to deal with were some of the residents of the community: the ones who believed that property rights trumped human right and guns are the law.

This was the first home in which it was impossible to make friends who lived closer than 14 miles away. We had friends in Grass Valley and Nevada City that we really liked, but getting together was always complicated. There was one neighbor who also built a home the same time we did. This was another time where I was always the "good" neighbor and invited them to visit often, but avoided at all cost any conversations that came close to politics or religion, government or firearms. Not too far away, there was a small "shopping complex." It included a gas station, a small grocery store, a vet and a few other small stores and a gym. I joined the gym and learned that they played only religious music and they played it loud. It was hard for me to relax and work out. I was more at home in that little cottage with the hippies than this gorgeous house on beautiful land.

You know that list you make when you have to decide something: pros on one side, cons on the other? We made that list, then remade it and made it again—always surprised how it turned out. We had our dream home with everything exactly as we wanted it: the furniture, the art and the views, all big pluses. Our studio/workshop building had been planned and executed to perfection. My kiln room never made my studio hot, my sink was large enough for big buckets; the trap underneath caught all the clay particles. I had a separate space for mixing glazes that kept all my toxic chemicals confined. A big worktable and my wheel faced our vegetable and flower gardens and the rolling acres of wild hay and grass beyond. Joe had every tool he needed, a rolling garage-type door for bringing in lumber and the same wonderful views that I had. Only our gallery and bathroom and the stairs that went to the second floor separated us.

And the best part of all of this was that, after a long day in clay and wood or oil paint, we had a sunken hot tub right outside our bedroom's French doors. The hot tub faced west and, with the open expansive views, we could watch the sunset every night of the year (except, of course, during storms and fog). The routine was to take a shower, prep dinner, pour a glass of wine and watch the sun set. Joe always in the hot tub, me often sitting on the side (too hot for a postmenopausal woman).

The kitchen was THAT kitchen: the one that was too big, the one that no one really needs. It had an island that was too wide for me to easily reach the middle to clean. All the surfaces were honed black granite. It looked more like slate. I loved that it didn't shine; I hated how hard it was to clean. The appliances were terrific, but I made a few design errors. The wall ovens were on the opposite side of the kitchen. That was not the original plan. I had meant to have a cook-top and oven together but some salesperson talked me out of that. The walk-in pantry had enough space to store five sets of dishes, every pot and baking pan ever invented and enough dry goods for years. I should have used some of that space for something else.

Cooking was terrific. I had windows and glass doors and skylights everywhere. During the day: sunshine, and in the evening: the full sky. We had mountains and pastures and no houses blocking anything. Stacks were my cooking favorites: many of them using southwestern and Mexican ingredients. An eggplant and salmon stack was popular: easy to make, healthy and tasty.
(See menu and recipes)

One dinner party that was not our usually fun group and rather odd was when Joe invited a few people from work. I knew all but one gentleman. The other guests were, in fact, more than work colleagues but friends. Joe must have shared our snake concerns. One new guest arrived with a gun and the intention of showing us how to shoot it and planning to leave the gun as a "gift." I put on my very best fake-gracious thank you and told him that I appreciated the gesture but we would be fine without the gun. Everyone else did their best not to laugh at the irony of the situation. I know our gun-toting guest was upset; he wasn't stupid. He could feel the vibes in the room. As big as the room was, it was hard not to see the look of surprise and amusement on everyone's faces. He put the gun away and we quickly changed the topic of discussion. The evening ended fine and I saw him a many other occasions with no sigh of tension.

The house was a draw for our son and his family. Our young grandson and his parents lived in San Francisco and welcomed the retreat in the country. We got to spend a lot of quality time with Ben when he was a toddler. It was also the time when we added a new member to our family: Griff, the Goldendoodle puppy. What a hoot he was and still is.

Our good friends lived in town. Unfortunately it was 14 miles away and not easy to casually stop by for a glass of wine but we did have lots of dinner parties just so we could see people. The parties were casual and fun but not often enough.

Joe was back to work, but I was alone with the dog, clay and my radio. Did I ever mention that I am an NPR addict? I have the radio on all day, up until we sit down to dinner.

We tried not to let all the negatives get in the way of our capitalizing on the positives. It was a wonderful lifestyle: working on our art and learning to be less dependent on having other people in our lives all the time. Joe's job was demanding, but easier than others to turn the pressure valve real low. He was getting better at just doing a great job but not at the sacrifice of his other interests. He started painting in addition to his furniture building, our gardening and daily hikes and lots of cooking. My anxiety about snakes, coyotes and mountain lions in our backyard became more rational: a healthy respect and a cautious distance from their usual habitats. And they seemed to be doing the same. The snakes never ventured, to our knowledge, onto our patio or in the house again. We built a deer fence around the four acres that surrounded the house and gardens, which kept the deer away. There were many days that, while I sat at my potter's wheel, I would see the coyote pacing back and forth by the back fence. It felt as if he was watching me. I actually started looking forward to his "visits." The mountain lion kept his distance.

Thinking about those years. Despite the social isolation, they were really wonderful. We both learned so much about ourselves and what our needs were.

We loved our Maine and Virginia retreats from our "real lives" and thought we could convert that way of life as our standard for our future. What we learned is that we are a little bit country and a lot city! The country life was a gift, but we missed the gritty energy more urban life gave us. For some reason, this life felt a bit too self- indulgent and I needed to be part of a community. Joe had a little of that at work and became very good friends with Mike who is still very much part of our lives. He lives in LA, but that doesn't keep us from being connected. Mike helped keep Joe sane at work, and I think Joe, in turn, did that for Mike.

Nature (snakes and heat), politics (not ours) and social isolation started us thinking about our new home. There was so much we loved, but we knew that years of this lifestyle would not work. So we put the "ranch' (realtor term) on the market and started looking in San Francisco and Berkeley. No problem finding like-minded politicos, lots of grit and energy there. The problem was that, for the price of our large ranch complex, we could buy a two-bedroom fixer upper. It took one year of bidding on and losing houses before we found a "good enough" house for the right price. The ranch sold for less than we had hoped, but the deal was clean and we did not look over our shoulders, not looking at what we left behind, as we drove down the 1/2 mile long dirt driveway to the mailbox and then down the road that would lead us out of "paradise" to urban chaos.

Our history told us that we tend to follow our hearts and are not afraid of change or adventure, so we were ready to start again. When we left Marblehead, we never looked back over our shoulders. It seems to be our pattern.

We had loved our home in the rural foothills of Floyd, Virginia. We had loved the life that our artist friends lived, so why not make that life style forever? We had picked a spot that reminded us of Floyd in beauty, quiet and isolation. What we forgot was that none of our Floyd friends lived in Penn Valley. So, on to the next reinvention of ourselves in the hopes that the next one would be just right!

Our studio, woodshop and guest apartment. The photo is a bit weird: colors and angle but you can see how spacious it was.

Great room with views of the Sutter Buttes. Those rocks outside the doors use to be home to a family of rattlesnakes.

Pottery made by Floyd, Virginia artists mixed with a mortar and pestle that came from Leon's drug store (my father-in-law). The plant was never on the counter. I have no idea who put it there for this photo.

First year of one of the gardens.

## BERKELEY, CALIFORNIA 2004-2009

Our new house was on a corner, three blocks from the University of California, Berkeley and the infamous People's Park. People's Park was the square block of grass where Berkeley students held their famous Anti-Vietnam War Protests. It is now home to drug dealers and the homeless. We traded our beautiful 46 acres for not much more than a courtyard. We traded rattlesnakes and coyotes for hard studying and hard drinking college students and an abundance of homeless people. There were apartment buildings and big old, wonderful brown shingle homes that Berkeley is famous for. Many had been converted into multiple units, but there were still some intact as single- family homes. Our house was still a family home, built in 1912, but not brown shingle. The previous owners did a kitchen remodel and it was thoughtfully executed, Most of the cabinets were original and the new ones looked much like the old ones. The appliances were all new and very high end and the counters marble and maple. There was enough storage and workspace and a beautiful extra large dining room that was made for large gatherings. The basement and garage had more than enough workspace for our art and woodworking and the driveway worked for our car. We were now a one-car family, living in the city where so much was walkable and public transportation was very accessible.

Walking Griff on UC Berkeley Campus

Our first two years, Joe worked part time and commuted to the foothills, which required an overnight in a motel. We both got ourselves involved in the art department at the University and were on campus a good part of our week. When not in classes, we were developing our abilities in our home studios. We met other artists and started the process of reinvention, again. Our neighborhood was rich with diverse and interesting people and a few problems. We had noise issues, crime and lack of respect for property. A beautiful tree lined street was often a mess with discarded trash waiting for someone to pick through and make the rubbish their own. A nice gesture for the homeless created an unsightly mess and health hazards. The noise was from students who felt they owned the neighborhood (usually only one group every year). The plus side of all of this was that these problems energized the neighbors who were concerned and we became a close, active and somewhat powerful voice. We knew the mayor, the chief of police on campus and in the city, and all the council people. Joe served on the board for People's Park and I was a health commissioner.

Back to the kitchen and food. Much of our regular entertaining was with wine and snacks while people met to discuss political issues in our living room. Once a month there was our co-ed book club, also with some of the same neighbors.

We did have another part to our social life, other than the artists and the progressive politicos, which could be exhausting. We belonged to a very fancy health club that was part of a resort, walking distance from our home. It had two outdoor swimming pools and countless other workout options. As swimmers, this seemed a perfect match for us. Here is where we met another group of people: professors, writers, "dot comers," businessmen, lawyers and politicians.

We were now walking in three worlds and loved it.

Each group: the artists, the neighbors and the health club crowd introduced us to their friends and our world widened. By nature, we are not big crowd people nor do we need to have a social event every week. In time, the numbers got smaller and smaller until we found the folks that we wanted as dear friends. Small dinner parties, casual dinners at restaurants, shared museum trips and walks meant the most to us.

When we were meeting so many new people, we thought about Sunday late afternoon cocktail parties. Big platters of cheese, roasted vegetables, salamis, seafood, wine and beer and a mixture of people from different parts of our life gave us an opportunity to join all parts of our life together. What we didn't know was the buzz about this "East Coast cocktail party idea."

Everyone thought it was so unique an idea and very East Coast. We were often asked, "Are you going to have another East Coast party?"

Twelve for dinner. Dishes are the ones I bought in Leavenworth. Table made by Joe. Flowers are real!

Our family has become larger and we now had moved full circle in our favorite form of entertaining. On the occasion that everyone was together, we sat around our dining room table and had make-your-own tacos, pizza or home made pasta (Joe's new talent. He makes ravioli, too) and sometimes a real roast chicken, potatoes, green beans for a Friday night dinner. Jonathan and Felicia and their two children, Benjamin and Sasha lived five miles away. Wendy, Matthew, Linden and Sky lived a 6 hour plane ride away.

Our dinners were simple: lots of vegetables, fish, chicken, tofu, rice and pasta. For Joe if you put tomatoes and herbs on it, he loves almost anything. For me, my favorite is sugar but putting that aside I am happiest with lemon, olive oil, and green herbs. I still liked putting together dinners with some extra pizzazz but still keeping the menu low fat. It was at this time that I discovered that garlic and I are not compatible. Friends and family have long lists of foods they do not eat but I do not think there is anything as difficult as garlic. In most restaurants and recipes, garlic is a given. Try eating out and see how far you get on a garlic-free diet. Indian, Italian, California, Spanish, and Mexican—all cultures that love garlic. I used to love garlic. No whining, it could be so much worse but it just makes me high maintenance and can be embarrassing when we go to someone's house for dinner.

While living in Berkeley, we started to travel again after many years of doing only small local trips and going to visit family. We had accumulated a generous amount of travel points on our credit card and were ready to cash them in. Our first trip was to Isla Mujeres in Mexico. We rented a large house and brought the three grandchildren (the 4th child was not yet born) and their parents. The house was on the beach and had a swimming pool. Each family had its own room and bathroom. It was perfect. Not a fantasy. It really was terrific.

Our next trip, Joe and I took our long awaited trip to Italy. We spent a month in Northern Italy starting in Venice and ending in Rome. Even with our food issues, we ate well. Joe continued to be strict about his fat intake and never liked garlic and I, the garlic lover, could never eat it again. The Italians were gracious and accommodating everywhere we went. We spent most of our time in small towns eating in neighborhood restaurants and each dinner was perfect. We immersed ourselves in art: ancient and contemporary. This isn't a travel journal, but we did bring home new ideas for our art, cooking and entertaining. Good quality olive oil drizzled on roasted vegetables was always a favorite, but now we knew it was loved all through Italy. We loved pumpkin ravioli with a simple broth, a dish we are trying to perfect. Pasta with a few slivers of black truffles and squid on pasta with a light red sauce are two dishes we are still working on. Notice I said "we." Joe is no longer making oatmeal loafs or boiling a carrot and a potato. He has become a serious cook and is cooking more than I am. It took some time for my ego to let this happen, but I am now pleased to be the one reading the paper while he cooks.

Our next trip was to Oaxaca, Mexico. We found a wonderful hotel walking distance to the two squares. We spent one day taking a cooking class. It was fun, but unfortunately we both got sick. We saw some other people from the class in town and some of them were sick too. We spent days exploring outlying small villages and going to artisans' homes: weavers, potters, and wood carvers. We usually do not shop when we travel but this was too tempting. We met a potter who was in her 80s, not well, but still working at her craft. We bought three wonderful pieces. We bought an animal from a wood carver that has now become a model for some clay pieces I have made.

Our next trip was to Paris. We rented an apartment for a month in the 6th district. It couldn't have been better. We were across from a butcher, baker, green grocer and wonderful neighborhood bistros (no candlestick maker). We ate at home or in the neighborhood. We walked and walked and walked. We went to every museum and gallery we could find. We went to all the parks, sat at cafes. What did we learn new about food? Nothing! At every café, restaurant and high-end grocer, the food preparation was just how we like it. The days of rich butter are either gone or not used where we went. The food was fresh and simple. There were sauces and they had some butter, but it was a hint and not the primary ingredient. We ate well. What we did learn was how little we really knew about art and that a month's crash course was just the beginning.

The frequent flier miles were almost gone but we felt the need for something different. We found a wonderful mid century, one story house to rent in Palm Springs for the month of February. We also found an artist studio that rented space by the month. It was ceramic studio but they made a space for Joe to paint. Every morning, we would walk the dog to the neighborhood park where there was a daily dog "party". We became part of this group that met again in the evening and sometimes continued back at our house for wine. In the morning after the dogpark and breakfast we were off to the studio for four or five hours of work. Around 2 we took a swim in our pool and late lunch, perhaps a nap or exploring and then back at the park by six.

Before we left for Palm Springs we told our friend who is also a realtor that we wanted to put our house on the "soft market." No advertising or open houses except to realtors, but she could spread the word. Before we left, we had the house appraised: we were ready to move on. We loved our five years, but were looking for something a bit smaller, less expensive and perhaps a bit quieter. See we were still struggling with the beauty, quiet vs. energy and noise issue. We can never get the balance right. The house in Palm Springs was just what we wanted in Berkeley. A walk-to location with easy access to everything but suburban beauty and quiet. Based on our love of the Palm Springs rental, we had a focus. After we sold the Berkeley house, we knew we wanted a one-story house with lots of indoor/outdoor access and lots of light. Everything happened faster than anyone expected. Before our month in Palm Springs was up, our house in Berkeley was sold, and we were renting it back until May. That gave us three months to find our next home. We put bids on four less-than-ideal houses. We lost all the bids. And then…we found a two-bedroom house with an very open floor plan, a wonderful dining room and kitchen. The kitchen design was great and the workmanship was superb. The basement/garage was perfect for our home studios—they just needed heat, electricity and better lighting. The kitchen, TV room and master bedroom all opened to a beautiful backyard. It was a block to a park and less than a mile to a village. So, here we go again. We get rid of stuff and pack what we want to keep, hire a moving truck, and drive two miles away from our interesting life in Berkeley to a more suburban life in Oakland, California.

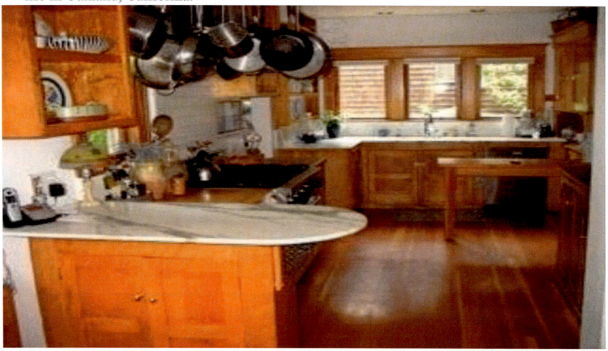

Berkeley kitchen
Yellow and green floral plate and yellow bowl from the 1940's Stangl Ware, New Jersey. My mother collected Stangl pottery. It mixes with pieces done by pottery friends.

Copper pots gone..stainless steel instead

Berkeley backyard

## OAKLAND CALIFORNIA 2010-2012
(on a foggy day and before we landscape)

Kitchen number 19!

Far wall had a great painting of Joe's but no photo after it was hung

Our studio space in the basement/garage.

This new home was really the perfect retirement home, we thought. It felt open and spacious and had no space that wasn't put to full use. The few steps between levels create interest and divide living use but yet are easy to deal with. No long stairways to carry groceries or laundry.

We quit our expensive health club and joined one that was less expensive and less crowded. We swam almost every day: outdoors, rain or shine.

Joe's art was getting a lot of recognition and he was painting all the time. He also began studying the cello, progressing beyond the squeaking stage.

My ceramics were also progressing and became a passion. I moved from wheel throwing to clay sculpture.

We discovered some wonderful walking spots and kept our 9 year-old Gooldendoodle fit. We lived in a family neighborhood with beautiful homes that were built after a massive fire in the 90's. Oakland, although infamous for crime, turns out to be a great spot for us. There is easy access to everything including a walk to a terrific Framer's Market and two blocks to Lake Temescal. The biggest event of this time was the birth of our fourth grandchild. Linden's brother Sky is an exciting addition to our family. Although PA. is a long trip away we all worked hard at keeping connected.

Linden, Sky, Wendy and Matthew at their home

Sasha, Jonathan, Benjamin and Felicia at a Wong family event

## RECIPES FROM 2000

Greensboro North Carolina
Kirkland Washington
Penn Valley California
Berkeley California and
Oakland California

We are healthy despite a serious bout of Giardia that forever changed the way we seem to be able to digest food. The diet changes again. This time, it is not by choice. It takes a few years before we figure it out and I am not sure how much of our changes have to do with the parasite and how much is just a digestive system that is in its $6^{th}$ decade. Anyway, we still love food and cooking. The century is now eleven years old and we have lived in Kirkland, Washington; Nevada City, California; Penn Valley, California, Berkeley and now Oakland. Each location had different food products readily available, except for Penn Valley. Food is an important part of culture. In Washington, fish was the mainstay of our diet. Better fish than Boston and that is saying something. The foothills of California—we never discovered what their food culture was, but everyone seemed open to new ideas and the stores were starting to reflect the beginning of an interest in fresh and diverse. Berkeley and Oakland, home to the concept of eating local, has outstanding farmer's markets. You can find one almost every day. The Berkeley Bowl and Monterey Market and the Monterey Fish Market and the Toki Fish Market rival any market anywhere. Eating well, no matter what your diet, is easy.

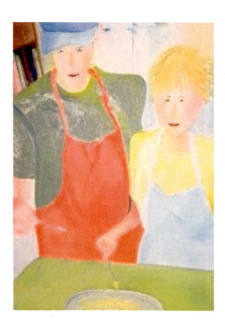

# TEA SMOKED CHICKEN

You may already know that I am a tea drinker from my many references to tea breaks in my memoir, but what I did not tell you is that my favorite tea is a smoky Lapsong. It is not easy to find, but worth the effort. When in Paris, I learned another reason to enjoy Lapsong. It is very low in caffeine. I hope that information is accurate. This chicken is made with my favorite tea. Note: this is another recipe that is without exact amounts. It is another by taste experience.

| | |
|---|---|
| Chicken breasts, boneless, skinless | 6 halves |
| Chicken broth | |
| Ginger | |
| Black pepper | |
| Lemon rind | |
| Lapsong Souchong tea | 1/2 cup |
| Brown sugar | |
| Bamboo steamer and wok | |

PROCEDURE:

1. Poach the chicken in chicken broth seasoned with ginger, black pepper and lemon rind. Do not poach until it is done. The chicken should still be slightly pink as it is going to cook another 12 minutes.
2. Line the wok with foil. Add the loose tea and brown sugar.
3. Put the steamer on top of the tea/sugar mixture.
4. Cover the wok and cook until it starts to smoke. Smoke the chicken about 6 minutes on each side.
5. Let it stand for a few minutes before serving so the juices stay in the chicken.

Serve with a lemon/ginger and soy sauce.

# HALIBUT (an excuse for using some ingredients that I love)

The ingredients for this recipe are a mixture of flavors that I use for many dishes. I am not able to include the exact amounts since I make it to my taste. Use the combination of ingredients and keep tasting until it tastes right to you. I have used these same ingredients in rice as a filling for stuffed grape leaves and also have added it to steamed greens and put on top of pasta.

Halibut              6 oz. per person
Coarsely chop and mix together:
Currants
Toasted pine nuts
Peel from one lemon or orange
Juice from lemon or orange
Fresh parsley
Fresh mint
Black pepper
Splash of olive oil

PROCEDURE:

Drizzle olive oil on fish. Grill or bake in 375 degree oven about 12 minutes until the fish is opaque in the center.
**wrap fish in large banana leaves before baking and bake in the leaves for an interesting presentation.
Divide the currant pine nut mixture as a topping for each serving.

This photo was taken in Mexico at a cooking class. We did not make Halibut or Swordfish.

# SWORDFISH

| | |
|---|---|
| Swordfish | 4 6 oz. steaks |
| Onion | 1 finely chopped |
| Raisins | 1/3 cup |
| Olives: black & green | 1 cup pitted and quartered |
| Capers | 1/4 cup |
| White Balsamic vinegar | 1/4 cup |
| Fresh mint | 1/4 cup, chopped |
| Fresh parsley | 1/4 cup chopped |

PREPARATION:
1. Season the fish with salt and pepper.
2. Brown about 2 minutes on each side in olive oil in large heavy skillet.
3. Reserve browned fish on a platter.
4. Sauté onions in skillet until golden. Add the olives, raisins and capers.
5. Return the fish to skillet.
6. Add the vinegar, mint and parsley and cook until fish is cooked through.
7. Serve with salad and rice:
    SALAD:
    a. 1 cup diced tomatoes
    b. 1 cup diced cucumber
    c. 1 cup diced avocado
    d. juice of 1 lemon
    e. handful of chopped mint or cilantro
    f. 2 Tbsp. olive oil
    g. salt and pepper to taste

## MONKFISH, FENNEL, TOMATO AND ORZO

| | |
|---|---|
| Monkfish | 2 lbs. |
| Fennel bulb | 2 large bulbs, chopped |
| Onion | 1 chopped |
| Tomato | 2 cups chopped |
| Fennel seed | 1 Tbsp. |
| Orange | 1 |
| Olive Oil | |
| Black pepper | |
| Saffron | 1 pinch |
| Orzo | 1 lb. |

:

1. Sauté the chopped fennel and onion is a large skillet.
2. Cover the skillet and slowly cook until the fennel is soft.
3. Add the 1 cup of diced tomatoes.
4. Peel the zest from the orange and dice and add to cooking mixture.
5. Squeeze the juice from the orange and add enough water to make 1 1/2 cups to 2 cups of liquid.
6. Cook the mixture until the tomatoes are cooked but still hold some of their shape.
7. Ten minutes before serving add the fish that has been cut into 8 pieces (two pieces per person).
8. Place the fish onto of the sauce and cover, cooking no more than 10 minutes.
9. While the fish is cooking, cook the 1 lb. of orzo and put in a bowl with olive oil to keep it moist.
10. Season the fish with salt and ground black pepper.

## FISH FILLETS WITH GREEN SAUCE

Tomatillo
Cilantro
Parsley
Mint
Garlic*
Jalapeno chili
Lime Juice
Cumin
Fennel
Coriander
Cloves

Halibut Fillets

White wine
Olive oil
Shallots

- This is one of those recipes that as I was making it I wrote down the ingredients but never the amount. When I made it a second time, I guessed.
- I think the combination of flavors is terrific and any amount you chose you will enjoy the preparation.
- Chop the tomatillos.
- Chop all the herbs and spices and mix with the tomatillos.
- Sauté the shallots in olive oil. Add 1/2 C white wine and poach the fish fillets.
- Serve the fish (and rice is good) with the salsa.

*I make it without garlic as I no longer eat garlic. I do not think this recipe suffers without it.

# VEGETARIAN HALLOWEEN DINNER

Appetizer:  Artichoke leaves with roasted red pepper dip
            Cheese selection and crackers


Dinner:

  Salad: mixed greens, fresh figs, roasted beets, goat cheese and pomegranate


  Entrée:
  Root vegetables, mushrooms, roasted chestnuts and seitan stew in pumpkins and polenta
  Season with cumin, coriander and black pepper with 1 cup of vegetable stock or mushroom broth

  Pumpkins:

  Hollow out small pumpkins. Place a small scoop of **p**olenta in the bottom of each pumpkin. Fill with the vegetable and seitan mixture. Bake 350 degrees until pumpkin is soft and the vegetables are hot. About 45 minutes.

  Couscous


Dessert:   Ginger apple pie
           Ginger ice cream and caramel sauce

   Apple pie is made with chopped crystallized ginger
   The ice cream is actually a high quality fat free vanilla frozen yogurt. I remove it from the container. Put it in the food processor with a large handful of chopped crystalized ginger. Process until smooth and creamy. Return to the freezer until time to serve.

   (You will know if you have a poor quality ice cream or yogurt if the amount is half of what you started with. Too much air in the product to make it look generous is my guess).

# MEXICAN INSPIRED DINNER

Appetizer:
    Spread made with chopped fresh figs, lemon, lemon peel, capers, and cilantro
    Chili oil roasted almonds
    Sheep and goat cheese selection

Salad:
    Arugula, corn, roasted red pepper, red onion, chipotle chili pepper, cilantro, lime juice, grilled shrimp and avocado
    Lime and mint salad dressing.
    Trader's Joes has a roasted corn that is frozen that has excellent flavor and is great in this salad.

Dinner:
    Chicken with tomatillo sauce and fruit 1
- 3 lb. chicken, quartered.
- Rub the chicken with salt, pepper and dried oregano. 3
- Refrigerate for 2 hours or 24 hours
  - Heat 2 Tbsp. of oil in large heavy pot.
  - Add chicken pieces and cook until brown, about 5 minutes on each side.
  - Remove to a plate.
  - Add and stir
  - 1 onion sliced crosswise
  - 2 garlic cloves, chopped
  - 3 Tbsp. minced chipotle chilies

Stir in    2 lbs. tomatillos, husked, & quartered
        1 cinnamon stick

Return the chicken to the pot. Cover and simmer, 35 minutes.

Add :    1 lb. pears, peeled, cored and cut into cubes
        4 oz. dried apricots
        3 oz. dried cherries

Simmer until pears are soft
    11. Serve with chopped green onions and fresh epazote leaves,

Corn tortillas
Brown rice
Steamed spinach

Dessert:
    Berry Sorbet
    Chocolate coconut bars

**Sorbet:**

Unsweetened frozen fruit (must be frozen)        4 cup
 I have used strawberries, peaches, berries, cherries and pineapple.
 Sugar     1/2 cup    Milk     1/2 cup
 I have used non-fat but buttermilk or any other milk like product works.

Flavors: I add 1 Tbsp. of lemon juice to strawberries, chopped crystalized ginger to peaches and cherries and rum to pineapple. Use your imagination.

Put all the ingredients in a food processor and process to smooth. Serve right away or freeze. If you are freezing you may have to stir the mixture every once in a while to keep it smooth.

**Chocolate and coconut bars**

    1 cup sweetened coconut
    1/3 cup sweetened condensed milk
    4 oz. bittersweet chocolate, finely chopped
    Mix coconut and milk together in a bowl. Melt the chocolate
    Line a 8" square pan with parchment paper. Put the coconut in the pan, spreading evenly. Pour the chocolate on top of the coconut.
    Chill 10 minutes

    Put the mixture on a cutting board and cut into 1" squares. Sandwich two squares together with the coconut in the middle and the chocolate on the top and bottom.

## GREEK DINNER MENU

Appetizer:
>Hummus: hummus without garlic is still good.
>>1 can chickpeas drained
>>juice of one lemon
>>cumin, coriander, black pepper and salt to taste
>>A few dashes of sesame oil or ¼ tsp. tahini. I learned to use sesame oil instead of tahini in Israel. It adds the flavor of sesame but keeps the texture less pasty.
>>Chopped parsley
>>Chopped cilantro (optional)
>>Puree the mixture. Taste for seasoning.

>Baba Gonosh:
>This is the same as hummus but instead of chickpeas you roast an eggplant and puree with the rest of the ingredients.
>I sprinkle the top with a few roasted sesame seeds. A mixture of black and white seeds looks great.

Salad:
>Arugula, artichoke hearts, roasted peppers and feta cheese

Chicken:
>3 lbs. chicken cut into pieces and browned in olive oil. Remove the chicken to a platter while you cook the onions.
>Sauté 3 cups of chopped onion for 5 minutes.
>Add: 6 whole allspice, 1 cinnamon stick, 1 tsp. cumin, 1 tsp. paprika, 1/2 tsp. nutmeg, 1/2 tsp. cloves and cayenne pepper to taste.
>Cook the spices and the onions for 1 minute.
>Stir in 1 28 oz. can of chopped tomatoes.
>Return the chicken to the pot (Dutch oven is perfect).
>Cover and simmer until the chicken is cooked.
>Add 2 Tbsp. of red wine vinegar, 2 Tbsp. of tomato paste and a pinch of sugar. Simmer until it thickens. Taste for salt and pepper.

Serve with a grain such as spelt or cracked wheat or rice and a green vegetable.

Dessert:
>Ice cream, assorted dried fruit and nuts and cookies

## "CHEF'S" DINNER

This dinner party presented an interesting challenge. First, both couples were about 30 years younger than we were, but that was no big deal. The big deal was their professional status. One gentleman was owner/chef of a very popular Italian restaurant well noted for its abundance of garlic. The second gentleman, is a recognized San Francisco chef and a vegetarian. He was the pastry chef for a famous vegan restaurant and authored the dessert chapters of its cookbook. His wife is an acclaimed painter. The wife of the Italian chef was a nurse. The dinner had to lack pretense, be vegan and be flavorful without garlic. There was cheese on the table but other than that everything on the menu was vegan and garlic-free.
Great wine helped.

APPETIZER:
"PA AMB OLI" (BREAD & OIL) WITH CHEESE
SICILIAN STUFFED ROASTED PEPPERS
- Roast small red peppers.
- Sauté assorted color peppers and mushrooms, finely diced.
- Add generous amount of chopped parsley, basil and oregano, and black pepper.
- Goat cheese normally but this evening I added a handful of panko.
- Heat before serving

OLIVES

CARROT, ORANGE GINGER SOUP

FENNEL ONION BISCUITS


**CARROT SOUP**

Serves 4 small portions

Ingredients:

2 Tbsp. butter
1 cup chopped onion
1 lb. carrots, peeled and diced
2 cup stock made from carrots, celery, onion, parsley and cloves
½ cup orange juice peel
from one orange
1½ tsp. cumin
1 Tbsp. honey
1 tsp. lemon juice
1/8 tsp. allspice

PROCEDURE:
1. Melt butter in saucepan.
2. Add onions and sauté.
3. Add carrots sauté until coated.
4. Add stock, juice and peel. Bring to a boil. Reduce heat, cover and simmer about 20 minutes.
5. Stir in cumin.
6. Remove from heat.
7. Puree in batches in a blender until smooth.
8. Return to pan, whisk in honey, lemon juice, allspice, salt and pepper.
9. Serve with yogurt.

# ONION AND FENNEL SEED BISCUITS

I have made this many times and I remember them tasting more of onion then fennel. I may have not used enough. The vegans did eat butter and did not mind small amounts of milk for baking. They were not that strict.

Ingredients:

7 Tbsp. chilled unsalted butter
1 cup chopped onions
¼ tsp. fennel seeds lightly crushed
2 cup flour
2 Tbsp. sugar
2 ½ tsp. baking powder
1 tsp. salt
¾ cup whole milk (I used non fat)

Oven 400 degrees.

Cover baking sheet with parchment paper.

1. Melt 2 Tbsp. of butter in skillet.
2. Add onions and fennel seeds.
3. Cover and cook until onions start to brown. (About 7 minutes)
4. Cool completely.
5. Whisk flour, sugar, baking powder and salt in bowl.
6. Cut in remaining butter.
7. Rub with fingers until coarse meal forms.
8. Add milk, tossing with a fork.
9. Mix in more milk if needed.
10. Gently stir in onion mixture.
11. Turn dough on floured surface and pat to 1 ½" thick.
12. Cut dough into rounds (I used a ½ cup measuring cup).
13. Bake 15 minutes.

## ENTREE
## EGGPLANT STEAKS

Slice eggplant into 2" thick slices.

Dip each slice in beaten egg whites.

Dip the egg white covered eggplant steak into panko breadcrumbs that have been seasoned with salt, pepper and any dried herb whose flavor suits your taste. (I like thyme and rosemary) Brown each steak in a fry pan coated with olive oil.

Bake the steaks in 400 degree oven until the insides feel soft but the breadcrumbs are crisp.


## PUMPKIN, BEAN AND MUSHROOM RAGU

Peel 1 small pumpkin. Cut the pumpkin into 1" pieces

Dice two shallots and sauté in olive oil.

Add 2 tsp. of white balsamic vinegar to the shallots and cook down.

Add the pumpkin to the pan with:
1 can of plum tomatoes (drained)
2 tsp. rosemary
2 cup canned cannelloni beans
2 cup vegetable stock
1 cup assorted sliced wild mushrooms

Cook until thick. I served the ragu in small hollowed out pumpkins.


## BROCOLLINI
Steamed and served with herbs and lemon juice

## SOFT POLENTA
Soft polenta is cooked much the way you make risotto. You slowly add water or broth and continually stir until the polenta is soft, thick and silky smooth.

## SOUR DOUGH BREAD PARMESAN CHEESE AND OLIVE OIL

# DESSERT

## FRESH FRUIT

## CHOCOLATE ALMOND CAKE

This is a recipe that I got from Bon Appetit Magazine. The recipe was cut out and I do not have a date but the recipe is credited to Dorie Greenspan and her Cookbook *My Home to Yours*. The recipe is not exactly they way sure wrote, I have made a few changes but the credit goes to her.

| | |
|---|---|
| Unsalted butter | ¾ C. |
| Flour | ½ C. |
| Cocoa powder | ¼ C. |
| Chocolate powder | 1 Tbsp. |
| Salt | !/8 tsp. |
| Egg whites | 6 |
| Light corn syrup | 1 Tbsp. |
| Vanilla | 1 Tsp. |
| Sugar | ¾ C. |
| Blanched almonds, ground | 1 C. |
| Bittersweet chocolate, fine chop | 4 oz. |

Preheat oven to 350

Melt the butter until it turns a light brown. Set aside to cool.
Mix together the flour, cocoa powder and chocolate powder and salt
Beat the egg whites until fluffy
Add to the egg whites : corn syrup, vanilla, and sugar.
Whisk the eggs until the ingredients are part of the egg mixture
Add the ground almonds
Add the chopped chocolate
Fold the flour mixture into the beaten egg white mixture.
Fold in the cooled brown butter.

Grease the sides and bottoms of two 8" round cake pans. Cut parchment to fit the bottoms of both pans.
Divide the batter between the two pans
Smooth the tops
Bake 25 minutes. Cool on racks, Peel off parchment paper.


Frost with Ganache and apricot jam

Ganache:

| | |
|---|---|
| Heavy whipping cream | ¾ C. |
| Bittersweet Chocolate | 6 oz. |
| Butter | 2 Tbsp. |
| Apricot jam | ¼ C. |

Bring the cream to a boil
Pour the hot cream over the chocolate
Whisk until smooth
Add the butter until blended

Put 2/3 C. of ganache in a heat- proof measuring cup.
Remain ganache put in a bowl place over ice to chill and harden.

Strain ¼ C. Apricot jam into a small skillet. Bring to boil
Spoon warm jam over the bottom layer of the cake and spread evenly
Let cool for 5 minutes
Drop cooled Ganache over the apricot and spread an even layer
Place second cake on top. If glaze is too firm microwave for a few seconds.
Pour the glaze over the cake, allowing the glaze to drip down the sides and the spread evenly.
Chill for 2 hours or more.

Cake can be decorated with almonds or apricots.

# PORK ROAST BIRTHDAY PARTY DINNER

Appetizer:
Antipasti: Caponata, roasted peppers, olives, goat gouda cheese, prosciutto ham and melon
First course: Baked stuffed artichokes

    Steam 4 artichokes until tender. Drain and cool.
    Cut each artichoke in half and clean out the choke.
    Sauté fine chopped shallot in olive oil.
    Add diced assorted wild mushrooms, cook to tender.
    Add enough panko breadcrumbs to make 1 cup of the mixture. Season with salt, pepper, parsley, basil and thyme.

    Place the 4 half's of artichokes in a roasted pan coated with olive oil (cut side up). Fill each artichoke with the breadcrumbs and sprinkle the top with olive oil. Bake about 20 minutes.
    Serve with olive oil and balsamic vinegar.

Roast pork:
    The day before, marinate the pork in: 2 Tbsp. tomato paste
        Chili flakes to taste
        1/2 cup orange juice
        2 Tsp. olive oil

    The day before, make the chutney:
        1 cup dried apricots, diced
        1 cup dried figs, diced
        1 cup pineapple, diced (I use frozen.)
        1/4 cup crystallized ginger, diced
        1 shallot, diced
        1/2 cup white wine or port
        1/3 cup brown sugar
        juice of 1 lemon
        rind of 1 lemon, diced
        red pepper flakes (to taste)
        cilantro (to taste)

Cook the above mixture for about 20 minutes. Refrigerate in a covered container.
Cooking the pork: Remove the roast from the marinade and throw the marinade out. Cut the roast in half lengthwise and open the roast like a book. Line one side with the chutney. Fold the top of the roast over the chutney and tie the roast with string to hold the two sides together with the dried fruit mixture in the middle.
Roast the pork at 350 degrees until the meat is 145 degrees.
Gravy: Made with sautéed shallots, port, 1 Tbsp. fig jam, 1Tsp. ginger marmalade, red pepper flakes, thyme and chicken stock or water. Cook until thickened.

Israeli couscous and Roasted Asparagus
Chocolate cake, whipped cream and raspberries

# THANKSGIVING 2010

Sage roasted turkey
        Madeira mushroom gravy
        simple stock gravy

Cornbread stuffing

Mashed potatoes

Puree of carrots, parsnips and squash

Green vegetable platter:
Brussels sprouts, green beans and brocollini

Sauce choices for vegetables:
    Lemon, mustard butter
    ginger butter
    olive, caper, herbs, lemon and oil
    shallots, mint, chili, lime and oil
    ginger, mint, lemon oil

Cranberry, orange and apple relish
Cranberry sauce


Pumpkin pie
Apple pie
Chocolate cake
Vanilla ice cream

## NEW YEAR'S EVE/ DINNER FOR 6

Appetizer platter:
    Smoked salmon, caviar, shrimp, brie, corn cakes, chopped onion, capers, lemon and sour cream

Dinner:

    Roast leg of lamb
        rosemary, garlic, thyme and lemon zest
    Herb roasted potatoes
    Cider glazed roasted root vegetables
    Sauté Swiss chard

These are all classic recipes and can be found in any cookbook and any web site. I have included this menu because it is so traditional and yet one of my favorites.

Dessert
  Chocolate cake with whipped cream and berries

Living in Oakland I thought my kitchen writing adventures were over. This is how I thought I would end my kitchen story.

> *So, what about the nineteenth kitchen... is it our last? It could be but you never know with us. It has all the room we need, it is efficient and has all the indoor/outdoor access we craved. We put in an herb garden, a rose garden and a cutting garden. They are all still in their infancy but we have done it before so we are confident, despite the awful soil and drainage problems that it will give us as much pleasure as that first little patch in Roxbury 47 years ago.*
>
> *Joe continues to cook but in this kitchen there is room for both of us. No more Beef Wellington or oatmeal loaves, but it is fun to take some of the classics and redo them to fit our current style of eating. Most of the time it works.*

I didn't know then when I wrote the end of my story that we had one major move and two more kitchens in our future! So the story continues.

# BALTIMORE, MARYLAND
## Churchill Street

While thinking about how I was going to bring this story to an end I was given a new beginning….

## KITCHEN NUMBER TWENTY!

Nineteen Kitchens seemed a perfect title for my reflections of cooking and moving. Our move to Oakland seemed to be the perfect place for this decade of us getting older and emerging as artists. We were going to stay. It met all our criteria: easy access to friends and culture, walkability, home the perfect size and aesthetic with a lovely yard allowing indoor and outdoor living, a place to do our art. And we were happy!

I had to change the title from its original "NINETEEN KITCHENS" for, despite how perfect the Oakland house was, we are now on a new adventure.

September 2011, my 93 year-old mother died. She had been living alone in Florida. We moved her two months before she died to Connecticut to be closer to my sister and her sons. It was a hard time, as illness and death has to be. A week after she died, our son, who lived three miles from our home in Oakland, told us that he and his family were moving to New York. The job changes for Jon and Felicia are thrilling and the experience for the children will be terrific, but it would leave us in California with no family. Fresh on the heels of my mother spending her last years alone, and family having to travel great distances to see her, gave us pause. Beautiful weather, a casual lifestyle, a terrific house, but no family…Family was a stronger pull.

Decision made. We were going to move. Where? Our daughter and her family are in Gettysburg. Our son and his family would be in New York. I won't bore you with all our ruminations, but after considering multiple options, we settled on Baltimore. It is less than two hours to Gettysburg and the fast train can bring you to NYC in about two and a half hours. We knew a few people in Baltimore whom we had not seen in 30 years or more (high school friends, medical school classmate and professional colleagues we have met along the way).

It has a terrific art community. It is less expensive than many other areas we considered. I was born in Maryland (Can one year of my life really count? I must have some pre-language hidden memories.), and all my mother's family were in Washington D.C. (long gone, however). So we settled into Kitchen Number 20 in the Federal Hill neighborhood of downtown Baltimore and our art studio is across two streets. We were in a very cool neighborhood and again trying to walk in as many different worlds as possible. Joe went back to painting, painting, painting and building furniture and I tried to find my voice in clay. We discovered that, like Berkeley, the neighborhood had some problems—many coming from an overabundance of bars and drunken young people. Also like Berkeley, the problems brought us closer to our neighbors and again to politics. We serve on many committees and continued to work with neighbors to maintain a quality of life for those who live here without sacrificing the spirit of the social life. Just looking for balance. This has brought us a wide circle of friends and has made our life rich with energy.

Food is another issue. The contrast of Northern California and Baltimore is apparent in most restaurants, but some searching and perhaps spending a bit more money we discovered some great places for that occasional splurge. The food markets are good, so we continued to be able to get wonderful produce and fish and did most of our eating at home. Like Kirkland, one of our favorite things to do when we feel like we need to be recharged is to walk three blocks to a bar/restaurant that attracts a more mature patron and have a drink and a salad and then go home for dinner. Old habits do not die they just get reinvented.

Interior brick walls from when this house was, in fact, a warehouse for coffins. No sign of its history beyond the brick walls. Couch is waiting to be re-covered. It has, since Marblehead, been yellow, so that is a possibility. Not sure.

Living room with view to open stairs that goes down to family room, grandchildren's bunk bedroom, laundry room, large storage closet, two-car garage and the front door.

Still finding a place to display some Ironstone and my Quimper. Can you see some of Julia's books?

# RECIPES FROM KITCHEN #20

## SALADS FOR A BUFFET:

Our first few months as we met people, we invited them for a drink and then walk to a local spot for dinner. By September, we were ready to really start entertaining. Our first event was a neighborhood potluck. The neighbors do this on a regular basis and we hosted the post-Labor Day party. Everyone brings a dish to share and a bottle of something to drink. My contribution was always something substantial so if there was nothing else we care to eat, we could count on my dish. Potlucks are hard for us. Everyone loves garlic, as I once did, so with my current inability to eat it, I am cautious. Joe is just fussy: fussy about fat, salt and what he calls junk. A standard for me is something where the major ingredient is a grain and then filled with what I hope are tasty additions:

1. A classic black bean and corn and cilantro salad that I add a generous amount of quinoa, roasted peppers and grilled shrimp.

2. Grilled chicken, cucumber and tomato and chickpea salad seasoned with tarragon or mint and parsley.

3. Couscous with chopped crystalized ginger, dried apricots, dates and white raisins (I use this mixture often). I like to season this with cumin and coriander and cilantro.

4. Roasted vegetable salad: eggplant, peppers, zucchini, capers, olives and sun-dried tomatoes mixed with a grain. (Cracked wheat is good).

5. Alternative to the above cracked wheat salad in the winter is to use roast root vegetables and season with warm spices instead of herbs such as cinnamon, nutmeg, coriander and cumin. I love ginger so I use it whenever possible and so it is almost always tucked in somewhere…root vegetables especially.

All the salads are dressed with lots of herbs or spices, black pepper, lemon juice and/or vinegar and olive oil. Goat cheese is great with the black bean salad, Parmesan with the roasted vegetable, and yogurt with the couscous and dried fruit.

# BUFFET DINNER PARTY

Our next event was the end of September. We invited 25 people, but because it was the same night as a Ravens football game, not everyone was able to attend. Who knew? I never thought to check the football schedule.

This was a group of people that we met or knew prior to our move. One woman was a classmate from high school whose older brother was my boyfriend for three years before I met Joe, and I had not seen since 1960. Another was also someone from high school but who also went to medical school with Joe and was his lab partner, whom we had not seen since 1967. One guest was in medical practice in Salem, Massachusetts before he moved to Baltimore and another did research with Joe when we lived in North Carolina. A close friend of our son at Bowdoin College had a dinner party for us when we were house hunting. Beside Eric and his wife, we met his in-laws and another wonderful couple in our age bracket that we now consider good friends. We also included a couple we never met, but had just exchanged informative emails with. She was the sister of a young man who is the father of our granddaughter's friend in California. And, of course our realtor and one neighbor. This neighbor invite was the exception because we did meet her before we bought the house. We had to draw the line with neighbors because the party would have been too large. The group was all ages and backgrounds and the food was simple.

No one knew everyone and very few had been to our home. Most lived in the suburbs and had to deal with finding parking and finding our house on a small alley where the street sign was hidden by one of the few trees.

I wanted to keep the food easy to eat. Most people would be standing. It still felt like summer and the menu was definitely summer fare.

Prior to dinner, I had an assortment of small bites around the house: in the family room on the first level, on the deck on the third level, and in the living room on the second. There was one guest who found the stairs difficult so I did not want to have the deck the main food spot.

The dinner was set out on the dining room table and everything was cold or at room temperature.

## COLD BUFFET DINNER MENU

**MOROCCAN STYLE CHICKEN BREAST** (tomato, soy sauce, orange juice, shallots, red pepper, coriander, cinnamon, cumin, fennel, ginger, vinegar and lemon)
    Artichoke hearts and Chickpeas

    **Stuffed Grape Leaves** (rice, pine nuts, raisins and mint)

**FLANK STEAK ROLL** WITH MUSHROOMS, SPINACH AND ONIONS

**SALMON, TILAPIA AND SWEET PEA TERRINE** (like a fish pate)

**EGGPLANT CAPONATA** (eggplant, celery, onions, tomato, olives, and capers)

**ROASTED SWEET PEPPERS**

**ISRAELI COUSCOUS and BARLEY BASIL SALAD**

**SAUCES:**
    CUCUMBER, MINT AND YOGURT
    HORSERADISH AND SOUR CREAM
    CHUTNEY

DESSERT:

**PEAR CARAMEL TART WITH CASHEW CRUST**
**APPLE CINNAMON TART WITH CASHEW CRUST**
**CHOCOLATE CAKE WITH RASPBERRY**
**CHOCOLATE GANACHE PEACH CAKE**

The evening was a huge success, much to my surprise. The food was fine, the house worked out and all the parking spaces we arranged with accommodating neighbors, who earlier in the day parked on the street, help to ease some of the stress. But what really made the evening fun was that everyone loved whom he or she met. People kept coming up to me to tell me about conversations that they had with someone new. I had been holding my breath for days for no reason.

Old Bay. Baltimore cooking is about seafood and Old Bay. In case you have not been exposed, this is a collection of spices that is mostly red pepper and paprika.
Many of the neighborhood restaurants are bars and the food is shrimp, crab, oysters and mussels—and Old Bay. My challenge in the kitchen is to use Old Bay but give it a personal twist. So far, nothing noteworthy.

**We are in our 7th decade and fifty years together**

**THANKSGIVING 2012**
Guest list:
Jonathan and Felicia and their children: Ben and Sasha
Wendy and Matthew and their children: Linden and Sky
(There are 4 vegetarians so vegetables and dairy protein are important)
Lots of crudities and my mother's cream cheese, olive and radish spread
Assorted nuts
Figs and goat cheese
Turkey
Chestnut stuffing (meat free)
Maderia and mushroom gravy
Lentil and carrot loaf
Spinach and ricotta pie
Roasted sweet potatoes
Mashed potatoes
Brussels sprouts with caramelized onions and lemon
Green beans
Chocolate cake, Pumpkin pie, Apple strudel and
Fresh fruit

## OPPS!!!

No sooner than I typed what I thought was the end ...
Here we go again!

## Baltimore, Maryland
### Warren Ave.

After kitchen number 19 I was sure the moves were over for a while and so my kitchen tale would end. Oakland was a wonderful home, but then we found ourselves moving to kitchen number 20 in Baltimore. We moved to wonderful large converted warehouse in the Federal Hill neighborhood near the harbor and all that it is good and edgy about city life. For sure, we were going to stay for a long time. But, two years later, we were getting ready for our next move. I never intended to add another chapter and thought even with this move the book would end at the nice round number of 20. But now I have more stories to tell and more recipes. It is not just about the new kitchen and it's remodeling; it is not just about food. The kitchen and food continue to be important, but this story is also about our remarkable dog.

First I will share a bit of back-story to put the story in context. Shortly after moving to Baltimore I learned that I have the potential to have some serious vision issues in the future. A diagnosis of macular degeneration is scary, but since I still had 20/20 vision and no symptoms, I gave it little thought. Joe, on the other hand, felt that if I do eventually have reduced vision our current home could be difficult to navigate. The four stories and the fact that the stairways are all open concerned him. After much discussion, the point that won me over to another move was that WE should make the decision where and when and not wait until the time when someone else (our children) would have to make it for us. We looked at condos all over the city and, after much research, ended back in our same neighborhood. The condo building used to be a furniture warehouse; it has twelve units and faces the park. The unit that was available is on the third floor with all but one window facing the park. It almost felt like the west side of Manhattan facing Central Park, of course on a very miniature scale. The price was much less than our budget, giving us cash to remodel a unit that had not been done since the early 1980's: kitchen and bathrooms were a must! So we bought it and the renters, wonderful new friends, were happy to accommodate our open-ended moving date as they had plans too.

Everything was falling into place until we learned that the condo association had a weight limit on dogs. The building has three little dogs. Our skinny, eleven year old goldendoodle was 12 lbs. over the weight limit. Everyone told us not to worry. They were all sure the co-op president would bring it to the board and it would sail through. Well, that didn't happen. We started relooking at other buildings, thinking we would just resell what we just bought. Nothing was as nice in our price range and buying something very expensive made no sense, so we felt stuck and a little angry.

Our kids offered to take him, but they each had their own dogs: our daughter with two and our son with one. Each family had two young children and all the adults worked full time. We didn't feel right adding more responsibilities to their lives. Some neighbors offered, but nothing felt right, until…

Our vet was on the lookout and contacted a woman who breeds "doodles." She knew someone and now, the heartwarming part of the story:

Three and a half years ago, a Baltimore woman, a professor and mother of four, was driving in Ohio with her two youngest while her husband and the older adult children were home in Baltimore. A truck driver for a major trucking company fell asleep at the wheel and hit their car head on. The mother died. One son had a crushed pelvis, and is now recovered and a college student. The younger son's brain injuries are permanent. With wonderful and sophisticated therapies, he has some language and can move one hand. Because his son is confined to a wheelchair and in need of constant care, his dad retired from his teaching position and is devoting his life to the care of his son. With a large part of the financial settlement, he has set up a foundation for families who have experienced similar tragedies but where there was no insurance settlement. He has set up a model home for handicapped accessibility and has made sure his son will be cared for the rest of his life.

Recently, he thought a puppy would be good for his son. The Labradoodle puppy is adorable and much like our dog was when younger: high energy. Realizing it would be some time before this dog would be a "service" dog for his son, he started thinking about an older dog. His breeder suggested he meet us and our dog.

We agreed to meet at our studio, which has a ramp and is handicapped accessible. As we were crossing the street to get to the studio, we saw the father and son were already there and waiting for us. As we got close, Griff looked at me and then gently tugged me closer to the wheelchair. As we got close, Griff put his paw on the young boy's knee and then his head on his lap. I was shocked. He had never been near a wheelchair and his usual greeting of someone he wants to meet is much more rambunctious. We all went inside and went to the small Ikea couch we keep in the studio. Griff never left the wheelchair until the father picked up his son so he could sit on the couch. Griff moved and sat on the floor between father and son. For two hours, he kept the boy close. Joe and I had no intention of giving Griff up that day. The plan was that if they wanted the dog, we would bring him when we moved. We looked at one another and without verbal communication knew we both felt the same. Joe went home and got all Griff's stuff. We knew that somehow Griff's 11 years with us were just the beginning for him. He was meant to be with this new family. We miss him terribly, but feel like proud parents that he is truly bringing some joy to the lives of a family that has had more tragedy then anyone should ever experience.

We get regular emails and photos and it is all still terrific. Besides the bond with the young boy, Griff gets to play with the puppy, sleep on furniture and eat people food. We think that one day, we might get a small dog…maybe.

Our house sold without going on the market. Six weeks of remodeling our apartment and it is now just right. We love the light from all the windows, the views of the park, the harbor and the city. It works except for sleeping space when the kids visit. No more bunk beds and privacy.

Cots, a couch that opens to a bed and sleeping bags or the Bed and Breakfast down the street are the choices.

A few photos of the twenty-first kitchen:

)

We have never strayed too far from our 1980's vegetarian diet, but now we are again looking at what we eat with a bit more seriousness. My macular degeneration diagnosis came with some interesting information. The doctors at Johns Hopkins believe that diet can slow the process down and suggested that I concentrate on eating lots of fish, dark green vegetables, orange fruits and vegetables, grains and broccoli sprouts. This was not going to be hard for me because these are the foods I like, but now I am refocused in trying to make these foods interesting.

The following recipes and the ones that I will end this book with are some of what we are eating in our seventh decade. Some of the recipes are my creations, some are from cookbooks, some from magazines and some from the Internet. Many I tweak to fit our needs, keeping Joe's low fat diet in mind and, of course, minus the garlic.

## COD WITH LEMON, PEPPER AND OLIVES

4 cod fillets, remove the skin
2 large lemons
½ cup green and/or black olives, chopped
1 red pepper, roasted
1 shallot, diced
1 tbs. small capers (if large, chop them)
½ cup fresh parsley
½ cup olive oil

Zest the lemons
Squeeze the juice and set aside roast
the pepper
    Heat oven to 450.
    Roast the pepper on all sides until it is starting to blacken.
    Put roasted pepper in a brown paper bag or a covered dish.
    When cooled, remove the skin and seeds.
    Very finely chop the pepper.
Sauté the shallots in enough oil to coat the pan and then add shallots to the chopped peppers.
Add the lemon zest, olives and capers and 1/4 cup of parsley.
Add 2 Tbsp. lemon juice and black pepper to taste.
Set sauce aside to stay at room temperature.

Oven 300 degrees.
Season the cod with black pepper and a small amount of salt (the roasted pepper sauce is salty).

Drizzle the fish with olive oil and the remaining lemon juice.
Slow roast the fish for about 30 minutes.

# CUMIN AND CORIANDER FISH WITH YOGURT

4 fish fillets (any firm white fish), skin and bones removed

2 tsp. ground cumin
2 tsp. ground coriander
¼ tsp. ground black pepper
¼ tsp. sea salt (or to taste)

Combine the three spices and salt in a small bowl.
Rub both sides of each fish with the spices.

Coat the bottom of a large skillet with olive oil.
Brown both sides of the fillets (about 2 minutes per side).
When golden brown, transfer the fish to a heatproof serving dish. Bake in 375 oven for about 5 minutes, the fish should be flaky.

Yogurt Sauce can be made in advance.

1 cup Greek style yogurt (fat free is fine)
¼ tsp. horseradish
1 Tbsp. parsley, chopped
1 tsp. dill

Taste and add more horseradish if you like.

Sprinkle the cooked fish with the remaining parsley and serve with the pepper olive mixture.

# SALMON

**STEAMED SALMON**
4 skin-on salmon filets
½ cup thin sliced leeks
½ cup thin sliced fennel
½ thin strips carrots
1 cup oyster or shitake mushrooms, thin slices
1 Tbsp. oil (peanut or olive)
2 tsp. toasted sesame oil (in the Asian food section)
1 Tbsp. soy sauce
cilantro or parsley

Steamer (bamboo or a metal one)
A wok or pan that will hold the steamer.
Sprinkle the fillets with coarse sea salt* and black pepper.
Add enough water to the wok to come up about an inch.
Bring the water to a boil.
Add the fish to the steamer.
Then add all the vegetables on top of the fish.
Cover and reduce heat so the fish steams.
Steam about 8 to 10 minutes.

Heat the oils and soy sauce.
When fish is ready to serve, pour the oil sauce on top.
Sprinkle with cilantro and/or parsley.


* Sea salt has a fresh sparkle to the taste and you need much less than regular salt to get full flavor.

## MISO SESAME SALMON

4 salmon filets
¼ cup mild white miso
½ tsp. unseasoned rice wine vinegar
2 Tbsp. maple syrup (optional)
*2 Tbsp. toasted white and/or black sesame seeds


Heat oven to 400
Mix the miso, vinegar and maple syrup in a bowl and blend.
Line a baking sheet with parchment paper.
Place the salmon skin side down on baking sheet.
Brush the miso mixture on the salmon.
Bake until the center of the filet is opaque.
Sprinkle the tops of the fillets with the roasted sesame seeds.

Serve with an herb flavored rice or grain and a steamed or ***roasted green vegetable


## SALMON EGGPLANT STACK

**Eggplant:** Cut into thick slices. Rub each slice with olive oil and rub with a garlic clove, salt and pepper. Grill.
**Salmon:** Marinate in lime juice, black pepper and olive oil. Grill.
**Polenta**: Cook the polenta adding parsley, oregano, salt and pepper. Put the cooked polenta on a cookie sheet or 9x13 pan and cool. Cut into rectangles. Grill (less than a minute on each side).
**Black Beans:** Cook, puree into a thick paste.
**Fire Roasted Tomato Salsa**: Buy your favorite. (Trader Joe's is good.) Assemble
on each plate:
    1 stack:
        1 eggplant slice
        2 Tbsp. black bean spread
        Salmon
        Salsa
    2 triangles of polenta sprinkled with cheese
        4 slices of avocado and a lime wedge
        A spoonful of sour cream
        Cilantro sprinkled over everything

# HERRING

I buy herring in white wine in the section of the market where they sell smoked salmon and smoked trout. I serve the herring with Greek yogurt flavored with dill and chives. It makes a lovely appetizer.


## PICKLED BEET AND HERRING SALAD

2 Tbsp. white-wine vinegar
1 tsp. sugar 1/4
  tsp. salt
2 Tbsp. extra-
  virgin olive
  oil
1/2 lb. pickled herring, drained
1 (1-lb.) jar sliced pickled beets, drained
1 (6 oz.) bunch watercress, coarse stems discarded (4 cups sprigs)
2 medium Belgian endives, cut crosswise into 1/2-inch thick slices (cores discarded)

Whisk together vinegar, sugar, and salt until sugar is dissolved, then add oil in a slow stream, whisking.
Arrange herring and beets on a platter and drizzle with half of vinaigrette.
Toss watercress and endives with remaining vinaigrette, then mound over herring and beets.

*Gourmet*
May 2005

# ROASTED TROUT WITH LENTILS AND VERJUS

**Lentils:**
2 Tbsp. olive oil
1 small carrot, peeled, finely chopped
1 celery stalk, finely chopped
1/2 small onion, finely chopped
1 cup black beluga lentils or French green lentils
2–3 cups low-sodium chicken broth
2 tsp. Sherry vinegar
Kosher salt, freshly ground pepper

**Verjus beurre blanc:**
1 small shallot, thinly sliced
1 whole star anise pod
1 bay leaf
6 black peppercorns
1 cup white verjus *Verjus is a tart juice made from unripe grapes. Find it at specialty foods stores and online* 1/2 cup dry white wine
1/2 cup (1 stick) chilled unsalted butter, cut into pieces
1 Tbsp. chopped fresh tarragon
1 Tbsp. fresh lemon juice
Kosher salt, freshly ground pepper

**Trout and assembly:**
2 Tbsp. olive oil
4 6-oz. skin-on steelhead trout or salmon fillets
Kosher salt, freshly ground pepper
1 Tbsp. unsalted butter
2 Tbsp. chopped fresh flat-leaf parsley

**For lentils:** Heat oil in a large saucepan over medium-high heat. Add carrot, celery, onion and cook, stirring often, until softened, 5–8 minutes. Mix in lentils and add broth to cover by 1". Bring to a boil; reduce heat, cover, and simmer, adding more broth as needed to keep lentils covered, until lentils are tender, 20–30 minutes. Mix in vinegar; season with salt and pepper. Cover and set aside; keep warm.
DO AHEAD: *Lentils can be cooked 1 day ahead. Let cool; cover and chill.*
**For verjus beurre blanc:** Bring shallot, star anise, bay leaf, peppercorns, verjus, and wine to a boil in a medium saucepan and cook until reduced to 1/4 cup, 15–20 minutes. Strain through a fine-mesh sieve into a small saucepan; discard solids.
Place saucepan over low heat and gradually whisk in butter, until butter is melted and sauce is emulsified. Whisk in tarragon and lemon juice; season with salt and pepper. Cover and set aside; keep warm.

# GREEK STYLE FISH

4 fish fillets (bass, trout or haddock)
1 large onion, chopped
1 red pepper, chopped
½ cup cooked artichoke hearts (optional)
1 clove garlic, crushed fresh
basil, parsley
1 Tbsp. capers
4 plum tomatoes, quartered
1 cup white wine
½ cup pitted black and/or green olives
olive oil

Heat a large fry pan with 1 Tbsp. olive oil.
Add onion, red pepper, artichoke hearts and garlic.
Sauté until the onion starts to wilt.
Stir in the wine, ½ cup basil and capers.

Reduce heat to medium low.
Add the fish and the tomatoes.
Sprinkle with salt and pepper.
Cover and simmer for about 5 minutes or until fish is flaky.
Add chopped bail and parsley and olives.
Serve immediately with lemon wedges.

# HALIBUT

The ingredients for this recipe are a mixture of flavors that I use for many dishes. I am not able to include the exact amounts, since I make it to my taste. Use the combination of ingredients and keep tasting until it tastes right to you. I have used these same ingredients in rice as a filling for stuffed grape leaves, and also have added it to steamed greens and put on top of pasta.

Halibut                6 oz. per person

Coarsely chop and mix together:
currants toasted pine nuts peel from one lemon or orange juice from lemon or orange
fresh parsley
fresh mint black pepper
splash of olive oil

PROCEDURE:

Drizzle olive oil on fish. Grill or bake in 375 degree oven about 12 minutes until the fish is opaque in the center.
**wrap fish in large banana leaves before baking and bake in the leaves for an interesting presentation.
Divide the currant pine nut mixture as a topping for each serving.

# HALIBUT WITH ZUCCHINI AND CARROTS BAKED IN PARCHMENT PAPER

1 large bunch of basil
¼ cup pine nuts 1
clove garlic
olive oil
lemon juice from 1 large lemon
rind from 1 lemon, chopped 1
cup shredded carrots 1 cup
shredded zucchini salt and
pepper 4 tsp. white wine

4 halibut fillets (6 oz. a piece)
4 large sheets (about 12x18) parchment paper

Preheat oven to 450 degrees.
Cut each parchment sheet into a heart shape that uses as much of the paper as possible. Brush each heart with olive oil.

In a food processor, grind the basil, pine nuts, garlic, and lemon rind.
Add 1 Tbsp. lemon juice and enough olive oil to make a thick paste (about 1 Tbsp.)

Salt and pepper each fillet and place it in the center of the heart.
Put about 2 tbsp. of basil, lemon paste on the top of each fillet.
Divide the carrots and zucchini equally on top of each of the 4 fillets.
Drizzle the remaining lemon juice on top the stack of fish and vegetables.

Fold the heart in half and seal the edges with crimping the edges (like a pie crust).

Place the packets on a baking sheet for about 15 minutes.
To serve: place a packet on each plate, cut a large X in the top.
Serve with a grain and extra basil and lemon.

# TROUT WITH HARICOTS VERTS AND ALMONDS

Four 10-oz. boned whole rainbow trout
8 oz. haricots verts, stem ends removed
Kosher salt and freshly ground white pepper
Canola oil
10 Tbsp. (5 oz.) unsalted butter
3/4 cup sliced blanched (skinned) almonds, lightly toasted
2 tsp. minced Italian parsley
2 tsp. fresh lemon juice

**To pan-dress the trout:** With scissors, cut away the dorsal fin along the back of each fish. Hold each pectoral fin (the one closest to the head) and cut away and discard the gill plate and pectoral fin. Turn the fish on its back and open it up. Starting at the head, cut away the belly flap on each side, along with the pelvic fin. Remove the tail by cutting across the fish about an inch from the bottom of the tail. Set aside.

**For the haricots verts:** Bring a large pot of generously salted water to a boil. Prepare an ice bath. Blanch the haricots verts in the boiling water for 2 to 6 minutes, or until they are barely tender, with a slight bite still left to them. Drain the beans and transfer to the ice bath to chill quickly, then drain again and dry on paper towels.

**To complete:** Lightly sprinkle both sides of each trout with salt and pepper. If you have them, heat two 12" nonstick pans (special oval pans work best for fish) over medium-high heat. If you have only one pan, cook two trout first, cover, and keep them in a warm place while you cook the final two. Coat each pan with a light film of canola oil. Add the trout skin side down and sauté for about 4 minutes on one side only. The fish may still look undercooked at the top of the flesh, but the hot ingredients that will top them will complete the cooking.

Meanwhile, put the beans in a sauté pan, add 2 Tbsp. of the butter and 1/3 cup water, and place over medium heat. Heat, stirring occasionally, until the water has evaporated and the beans are hot and glazed with butter. Season to taste with salt and pepper. Remove the pan from the heat and keep warm.

When the fish are done, cut off the heads and discard, if desired, and place the fish on serving plates. Drain the oil from one of the pans and return the pan to the heat. Add the remaining 8 Tbsp. butter and a pinch of salt to the hot pan. When the butter begins to brown, add the almonds, shaking the pan to brown them evenly. When they are a rich golden brown, add the parsley and lemon juice.

Meanwhile, cover each trout with one-quarter of the beans.
Spoon the foaming butter and almonds over the haricots verts and around the edges of the plates.

*Bouchon* by Thomas Keller
October 2004
*When we lived in Northern California, this was our favorite restaurant and still continues to be our best dining experience.*

# TROUT WITH PRESERVED LEMON VINAIGRETTE

This recipe comes from Chef Viet Phem, Salt Lake City Utah. He was profiled in the March 2014 issue of Food and Wine.

3 Tbsp. cider vinegar
2 Tbsp. lemon juice
2 Tbsp. minced preserved lemon peel
1 Tbsp. minced shallot
1 ½ tsp. fish sauce
1 tsp. sugar
½ cup grape seed oil
1 Tbsp. chopped parsley
Kosher salt and freshly ground pepper
Six 6- oz. trout fillets

Whisk the vinegar, lemon juice, preserved lemon and minced shallots, fish sauce and sugar together.
Add ¼ cup oil.
Stir in the chopped parsley and season the vinaigrette with salt and pepper.

Season the trout with salt and pepper.
In a large skillet heat 2 Tbsp. oil.
Add 3 trout fillets, skin side down, and press with a spatula to flatten. Cook over high heat until the skin is crisp. About 3 minutes
Flip the fillets and cook until the flesh is just white, about 30 seconds. Repeat
with the other three fillets.

Set the trout on plates, skin side up, and top with watercress.
Spoon some vinaigrette over the fish and watercress. Serve with the remaining vinaigrette.

# TUNA KABOBS

½ lb. potatoes (sweet potatoes or white) cut in half
1 lb. tuna, cut into 1 in. pieces
6 olives, pitted and chopped
1 pint small tomatoes (grape or cherry tomatoes)
1 red pepper, cut into 1". pieces
1 zucchini, cut into ½ ". rounds
1 yellow squash, cut into ½ " rounds
4 tsp. Dijon mustard
1 tsp. horseradish
2 tsp. lemon juice
4 Tbsp. olive oil
Salt and pepper
½ cup plain Greek yogurt (fat free is fine)
1 bunch arugula

8 wooden skewers that have been soaked in water or stainless steel skewers

Preheat the oven to 400 degrees.

Beat together the mustard, horseradish, olive oil and lemon juice. Divide the dressing in half.

Pour half the dressing over the tuna cubes, tomatoes, pepper, zucchini and squash making sure all the pieces are coated.

Steam the potato cubes for about 10 minutes. (Sweet potatoes cook faster than white potatoes.) Drain.

Line a baking sheet with a light coating of olive oil.
Place the tuna, potatoes and vegetables on the skewers, alternating so that they include equal amounts of everything and the colors are interesting.

Cook in the hot oven until the fish is done and the vegetables start to brown. This can also be done on a grill.

Add the yogurt to the remaining dressing.

Put a pile of arugula on each plate, place two to the skewers on top of the salad.

Sprinkle the olives around the plate and then spoon a small amount of dressing over the fish. If there is extra dressing, bring it to the table with some lemon wedges.

## BUTTERNUT SQUASH/SWEET POTATO CAKES WITH SMOKED SALMON

1 lb. butternut squash peeled and shredded
Use a food processor if you have one. If not you can use a metal grater.
1 lb. sweet potatoes, peeled and shredded
1 small onion, shredded or finely chopped
½ cup flour or cornstarch
2 eggs
salt and pepper to taste
Combine all the ingredients.

Brown in a fry pan with enough oil to coat the pan. (optional)

Heat on a parchment lined cookie sheet until cooked (about 15 minutes to 20 minutes depending on if they were precooked in a fry pan).

Serve with sour cream and smoked salmon.

## ROASTED CARROTS WITH YOGURT

3 lbs. carrots, peeled and cut into bite size pieces
1 orange, grate the peel and then juice the orange
1 Tbsp. thyme
¼ cup olive oil
1 tsp. ground coriander
1 tsp. ground cumin
1 cup Greek yogurt
¼ cup chopped cilantro leaves

Preheat oven 425 degrees.

Toss carrots with orange juice, orange peel, thyme and olive oil

Spread evenly on parchment lined baking sheet.

Bake 30 minutes.

Add coriander, cumin and cilantro to yogurt.
Season with salt and pepper. Serve carrots with yogurt

# ROASTED SWEET POTATO SLICES

1 Tbsp. olive oil
3/4 pound sweet potatoes, scrubbed, left unpeeled, and cut into 1/8"thick slices coarse
salt for sprinkling on the potatoes

Brush the potato slices with olive oil and sprinkle each with salt and pepper to taste. Arrange the potato slices, not touching, in rows on a baking sheet lined with parchment paper. Roast the potatoes in the upper third of a preheated 450°F. oven, turning them once. Bake until they are golden and crisp.

## Sweet Potato and Kale Pizza

1 medium sweet potato, peeled and cut into 1/2" cubes
1 1/2 Tbsp. olive oil, divided
1/8 tsp. crushed red pepper flakes
1 package (21 oz.) prepared whole-wheat pizza dough
1 bunch curly kale, stemmed and torn into bite size pieces
1/4 cup crumbled goat cheese
2 Tbsp. shredded parmesan
1 Tbsp. crushed walnuts

Heat oven to 425°F. Boil a large pot of water. Cook potato in water until fork-tender, 7 to 10 minutes. Remove from heat, drain and let cool 5 minutes. In a food processor, pulse potato, 1 Tbsp. oil, red pepper and a pinch of salt until sauce is smooth. Roll out dough until ¼" thick. Spread potato sauce evenly over dough. Toss kale in remaining 1/2 Tbsp. oil; top pizza with goat cheese, kale and parmesan. Bake until crust is golden, 10 to 15 minutes, sprinkling on walnuts in final 2 minutes.

*Self Magazine*
September 2013

## SWEET POTATOES WITH ORANGES AND NUTS

1 1/2 lb. sweet potatoes, cut into bite size pieces
2 tbs. chopped nuts (pistachios, cashews or pecans)
3 Tbsp. chopped cilantro or parsley
2 tsp. grated fresh ginger
1 orange, juice and zest
2 tsp. olive oil
Salt and pepper

Lightly coat the potato cubes in olive oil. Roast in a 400 degree oven until they are tender and slightly brown.

Place the potatoes in an ovenproof serving dish.
Gently mix the remaining ingredients with the potatoes using a wooden spoon. Heat at 350 degrees for 15 minutes.

### SWEET POTATO PANCAKES:
Mix together:
- 2 grated yams
- 1 grated russet
- ½ c. flour
- 2 egg whites
- salt and pepper

Form into cakes and brown in oven or in a heavy skillet. Serve with a tomato salsa for a unique taste combination.

# SWEET POTATO SPREAD

vegetable oil cooking spray
3 large sweet potatoes (about 2 lb.), peeled and cut into 1" cubes
2 medium carrots, peeled and finely chopped
1 small yellow onion, chopped
2 Tbsp. tahini
3/4 tsp. salt
1/4 tsp. curry powder
1/4 tsp. ground cumin

Heat oven to 400°F. Coat a shallow roasting pan with cooking spray; cook potatoes (covered with foil) for 15 minutes. Uncover and roast until tender, about 30 minutes. Meanwhile, bring carrots, onion and 1/2 cup water to a boil in a medium nonstick skillet. Reduce heat; simmer, covered, 5 minutes. Uncover; cook until water evaporates and vegetables are tender, about 3 minutes. In a food processor, process potatoes with remaining ingredients until smooth. Add just enough water to make a spreadable paste, about 1 cup. Add carrot mixture; pulse until blended. Serve at room temperature or chilled, with whole wheat pita wedges.

*SELF Magazine*
November 2005


## PUMPKIN, BEAN AND MUSHROOM RAGU

Peel 1 small pumpkin. Cut the pumpkin into 1" pieces.

Dice two shallots and sauté in olive oil.

Add 2 tsp. of white balsamic vinegar to the shallots and cook down.

Add the pumpkin to the pan with:
1 can of plum tomatoes (drained)
2 tsp, rosemary
2 cup canned cannelloni beans
2 cup vegetable stock
1 cup assorted sliced wild mushrooms

Cook until thick. I served the ragu in small hollowed-out pumpkins.

# BEET BURGER

3 cups of cooked beets.
    (The golden beets work best in this recipe but may not have all the health benefits of the red beets.)
½ cup chopped nuts (cashews, almonds or walnuts)
½ cup cooked grains (rice, cracked wheat, barley…great way to use leftovers)
1/2 cup panko bread crumbs
1 egg
2 egg whites
Season to taste with: thyme, parsley, tarragon or mustard and horseradish salt and pepper

Mix all the ingredients together.
Form 6 patties.

Cooking options:

*Place the 6 patties on a parchment lined cookie sheet and bake at 400 degrees until they are firm and golden (about 20 minutes).

*Heat a large pan with 1Tbsp. oil and cook the patties to brown. After the 6 are browned, heat them in a 400 degree oven on a parchment lined cookie sheet for about 15 minutes.

Serve on a hamburger bun with lettuce, tomato and avocado.

# CARROTS AND ORANGE

Ingredients:

2 Tbsp. butter
1 cup chopped onion
1 lb. carrots, peeled and diced
2 cup stock made from carrots, celery, onion, parsley and cloves
½ cup orange juice
peel from 1 orange 1
½ tsp. cumin
1 Tbsp. honey
1 tsp. lemon juice
1/8 tsp. allspice

PROCEDURE:

    Melt butter in saucepan.
    Add onions and sauté.
    Add carrots sauté until coated.
    Add stock, juice and peel. Bring to a boil. Reduce heat, cover and simmer about 20 minutes.
    Stir in cumin.
    Remove from heat.
    Puree in batches in a blender until smooth.
    Return to pan, whisk in honey, lemon juice, allspice, salt and pepper
    Serve with yogurt.

# BUTTERNUT SQUASH AND APPLES

1 butternut squash: skin and seeds removed. Cube the flesh
1 shallot, diced
1 crisp apple, peeled and diced
1 Tbsp. rice wine vinegar or white balsamic vinegar
1 tsp. thyme 1
Tbsp. butter
salt and pepper


Oven 400.
Place the squash cubes on a lightly oiled baking sheet.
Roast until they are tender.

Melt the butter in a skillet.
Add the shallots and cook until they start to soften.
Reduce the heat to medium.
Add the apples and cook, stirring so they do not burn. (Add a drop of water or butter if the pan seems too dry. The apples should give off a bit of liquid.)
Once the apples start to soften, add the vinegar and cook until it evaporates. Season with thyme, salt and pepper.

When the squash cubes are soft, add them to the seasoned apples and serve. This can be made ahead and reheated.

# CAULIFLOWER AND CARROT PUREE

You can think of this dish as a substitute for mashed potatoes. It is very nice as a base for stews. Put the puree on the plate and then the stew on top of the puree. It makes an interesting contrast and the puree is very easy and fast to make.

1 head of cauliflower, broken into chunks
3 peeled carrots, cut into fourths
1 medium onion, chopped
3 Tbsp. olive oil
salt and pepper

Sauté the onion in ½ Tbsp. olive oil.
Steam the carrots and cauliflower until they are soft.
Mix the onion and vegetables in a food processor and puree, adding the remaining olive oil.

Salt and pepper to taste.

I have kept the seasoning to a minimum as I usually use this to accompany more highly seasoned food. If you are using it as a dish on its own, you can add any herbs or even grated cheese.

# COOKING GREENS

Greens are quick and easy to cook. They can be flavored to fit almost any cuisine. The secret is to cook them quickly with as little liquid as possible.

Greens that are commonly available, eye healthy and delicious:
**Collard Greens Escarole Kale Mustard Greens Spinach Swiss Chard Turnip Greens Bok Choy**
Keep in mind when you purchase greens for cooking that they all cook down to a much smaller amount than you might expect. I figure about 1 lb. for two people as a side dish.

PREPARATION:
If the greens are young, small and tender, the only preparation is to clean.

If the greens have a coarse stem running down the middle, fold the green in half and remove the stem.

With larger greens, how you cut them depends on the use. The following are a few choices:
- Coarsely tear the leaves with your hands.
- Roll a cluster of leaves, one on top of another, into a cylinder and then slice.
  - This gives you even strips.
- Chop with a cleaver.
- Leave whole.

Cooking methods:

Steam: Put the greens in a steam basket. Place the basket in a pot with water making sure the bottom of the steamer does not touch the water. Cover the pot. Bring the water to a boil. Turn the temperature very low and watch the greens. Remove from heat as soon as they wilt. This could take as quick as a minute depending on the greens and the size of the pot.

Sauté: Put enough oil to lightly coat the bottom of a fry pan that is large enough to hold the greens. Heat the pan, add the greens and stir with a wooden spoon until all the greens wilt.

If the greens are going in a soup, add them just before serving.

Roast: Try roasting as an interesting change. Spread the greens on a baking sheet lightly oiled. Sprinkle with salt and pepper. Roast in a 400 degree oven until they reach the doneness you like. I like them crisp.

## ESCAROLE, KALE AND BOK CHOY

We usually think of escarole as a salad green but it is also great as a cooked side dish. This recipe has a slight Asian influence.

1 head escarole
> Clean the escarole by cutting out the center stem and trimming the ends. Cut the leaves into slices.

1 bunch kale
> Clean the center stem, cut into strips.

1 bunch bok choy Clean and slice.

1 small onion diced
2 celery stalks, sliced
2 carrots, cleaned and sliced
1 lb. assorted wild mushrooms, cleaned and sliced
1 slice ginger, diced
1 Tbsp. toasted sesame oil
1 Tbsp. canola oil
1 Tbsp. toasted sesame seeds
Soy sauce to taste

Add the two Tbsp. of oil (sesame and canola) to a wok or large fry pan.
Add the onion to the oil and cook until it is translucent. Add the ginger, the mushrooms, celery and carrots and cook until they are tender but not soft.
Remove to a platter.
Quickly cook the greens until wilted. Add the greens to the mushroom mixture. Stir in a splash of soy sauce.
Sprinkle sesame seeds on the top. Serve immediately.

# ROASTING VEGETABLES

Broccoli is usually steamed or stir-fried or served raw, but a new way to cook most vegetables is to roast them in the oven. When you roast a vegetable, you do not lose any of the nutrients to the water nor do you need to use excessive oil as in stir-frying. And, best of all, it is easy. Once the vegetables are roasted, you can then use them in any way you normally would. but the big secret is that roasting brings out so many of the natural flavors that the vegetables are great right out of the oven.

The standard method I use is to line a baking sheet with parchment paper, which makes clean up a snap, but if you don't use the paper then just brush a small amount of oil on the bottom of the pan. Be careful not to use too much oil so the vegetables do not become soggy.

Preheat the oven 400 degrees.

Cut and clean the vegetables to the size you want.
The following are a few examples:

<u>Brussels sprouts</u>, I cut in half.
<u>Broccoli,</u> I cut into good size florets.
<u>Carrots,</u> Depends on their use, but most often I cut the carrot in half and then each of those halves into quarters, making thick strips.
<u>Green Beans,</u> Just cut the stems off.
<u>Cauliflower,</u> Florets.
<u>Eggplant,</u> Thick slices.
<u>Butternut squash,</u> Peeled and cut into chunks.
Etc.

After you clean and cut the vegetables toss, them with a small amount of olive oil and any seasoning that works for your use. Salt and pepper if you like.

Spread the vegetables on the baking sheet and roast until they are crisp tender for the green vegetables and soft for the squash and eggplant.

## SAUTEED BRUSSELS SPROUTS WITH ALMONDS AND CURRANTS

2 Tbsp. or olive oil
1 Tbsp. minced shallot
12 large brussels sprouts (about 1 1/2 lbs.), trimmed, leaves separated from cores (about 8 cups), cores discarded
3/4 cup shelled unsalted almonds or pistachios
¼ cup currants
2 Tbsp. fresh lemon juice

Heat oil in large nonstick skillet over medium-high heat. Add shallot and stir 20 seconds. Add Brussels sprouts and cook until they are tender but not too soft. And still dark green ( about 3 minutes)
Add the nuts and currants.
Drizzle lemon juice over the sprouts, nuts and currant.
Season to taste with salt and pepper.


## STUFFED KALE

.
Tuscan Kale, 1 large bunch
2 lbs. plum tomatoes, cut in half and roasted
1 large onion, chopped
½ lb. mushrooms, chopped
Herbs: 1 tsp. thyme, ¼ tsp. rosemary and 1 tsp. parsley
½ cup pignoli nuts (optional)
1 cup cooked quinoa or spelt
Goat cheese

Oven 400 degrees.
Sprinkle the tomatoes with olive oil, salt and pepper.
Roast until they are soft, about 15 minutes.
When they are roasted, coarsely chop and taste for seasoning. Add herbs if you like.
While the tomatoes are roasting, clean the kale and cut off the lower stem.
Steam the kale in hot water until the leaves are soft enough to roll.
Sauté the onion and mushrooms in olive oil. Cook until soft but not mushy.
Add the herbs and the mushrooms and onions to the cooked quinoa.
Season the quinoa with salt, pepper and nuts if you like.
Place a heaping Tbsp. of quinoa on each leaf of kale. Roll and place it in an oiled baking dish.
Cover the baking dish with foil. Heat at 350 degrees until they are hot (about 20 minutes). Serve topped with a spoonful of tomatoes and a small slice of goat cheese.
This is a nice side dish with fish and butternut squash…nice colors, texture and taste.

# SALADS

For me, a salad is the staple of my diet: for lunch or to start the dinner. It does not have to be a dish for a diet. It can be filled with protein and even carbs, but for me it is mostly about greens, vegetables and fruit and some protein. It is also a wonderful way to reconvert the leftovers from last night's dinner. Depending on the ingredients and/or my mood, I make a chopped salad or arrange the ingredients on a dinner plate. The chopped salad is simply taking all the ingredients and coarsely chopping them. Mix them together and add the dressing. The advantage to this is that with each bite you get a mixture of the ingredients. An arranged salad is usually more attractive and the advantage is that you get to taste each ingredient separately.

Salads, like stews, are a great way to use your imagination and express your individuality.

The following is my list of possible ingredients and combinations that I like:

Start with the greens. The darker the green the better for you and the richer the taste. My three favorites are:

**Kale** All varieties, but I love the small baby kale. If you use large kale leaves, cut out the center stem.
**Spinach**. The baby spinach is easier to clean and better in salads.
**Arugula**

After you chose your greens, and combining more than one makes the salad more interesting, the next step is the protein. Some eye healthy choices:

**Fish:** I use fish left over from dinner, canned tuna, smoked trout and herring.

**Chicken or turkey:** I will often cook extra chicken breasts and freeze them. The frozen cooked chicken breasts taste fine reheated and chopped in a salad.

**Eggs:** Hard-boiled eggs keep for a few days in the refrigerator. I sometimes will mix a hard boil egg with some canned tuna.

**Cheese:** You will notice that there is not a lot of cheese in this cookbook. I think there are better ways to get protein but I also love cheese. I just use it sparingly.
For example: feta cheese, honey crisp apples and trout is a terrific combination...a bit salty but good.

**Fruits and Vegetables:** The reason that I pick my protein first is I like certain vegetables and fruit to go with different proteins. Crisp apple chucks are a great balance to fish. Sweet ripe pears are also wonderful. Grapefruit and oranges go nicely with arugula. Broccoli sprouts go on every salad.

Try to include some of the following:

**Broccoli sprouts**
**Carrots**
**Brussels sprouts, sliced fine or shaved**
**Broccoli**
**Green beans**
**Beets**
**Red pepper ( roasted is great)**
**Slices of oranges or grapefruit**
**Dried apricots**
**Roasted nuts ( I use unsalted)**

**Dressing:**

**Lemon juice.** A great way to get your citrus and what I think makes a great dressing. I use the juice of 1 lemon for 1/2 cup of olive oil. You can add your favorite vinegar and more oil to suit your taste.

**Olive oil**

**Flavorings**:
Mustard
Horseradish
A combination of dry and fresh herbs and spices. I think in clusters of three.
  For example:
    basil, oregano and parsley
    thyme, rosemary and parsley
    cumin, coriander and cilantro
    dill, mint and thyme
    tarragon , rosemary and lemon peel

Sea salt and pepper to taste.

## KALE & BRUSSELS SPROUT AND CHINESE CABBAGE SALAD

1/4 cup fresh lemon juice
2 Tbsp. Dijon mustard
1/4 tsp. sea salt, plus more for seasoning
Freshly ground black pepper
½ cup olive oil

2 large bunches of kale (baby kale if available). If using large kale, cut out the center stem, roll the kale and slice.

12 oz. brussels sprouts, trimmed, finely sliced.
One large Chinese cabbage sliced to match the size of the kale slices.

Combine lemon juice, Dijon mustard, 1/4 tsp. salt, and a pinch of pepper in a small bowl of oil. Stir to blend; set aside to let flavors meld. Mix thinly sliced kale and shredded brussels sprouts and cabbage in a large bowl.
Add dressing to kale mixture. Taste for seasoning.


## ROASTED BRUSSELS SPROUT AND APPLE SALAD
1 Tbsp. plus 1 tsp. olive oil, divided
1 pound Brussels sprouts, halved lengthwise
1 apple, cut into 1/4" slices
1 yellow onion, cut into 1" chunks
1/4 cup tahini
2 Tbsp. rice wine vinegar
1 Tbsp. pure maple syrup
2 tsp. white miso
1/8 tsp. crushed red pepper flakes
1/2 cup hazelnuts, finely chopped
4 cups baby spinach
1/2 cup crumbled blue cheese

Heat oven to 400°F. Grease a baking sheet with 1 tsp. oil. In a bowl, combine Brussels sprouts, apple, onion and remaining 1 Tbsp. oil; toss to coat. Roast on baking sheet, turning once, until sprouts are brown and tender, 25 to 30 minutes. In a bowl, whisk together tahini, vinegar, syrup, miso, red pepper and 1/4 cup plus 1 Tbsp. water until smooth; set aside. Heat a large skillet over medium heat. Toast hazelnuts 3 to 5 minutes, stirring occasionally. Divide spinach, sprout mixture, hazelnuts, blue cheese and tahini dressing among 4 plates. Season with salt and black pepper.

## SPELT AND CHICKEN SALAD

1 cup spelt (or farro or any other grain that holds it shape)
2 skinless, boneless chicken breasts
2 carrots, cut into matchsticks
3 plum tomatoes, cut into fourths
1 bunch Tuscan kale, ribs and stems removed and coarsely chopped
6 Tbsp. olive oil
2 Tbsp. lemon juice
2 Tbsp. grated parmesan cheese
¼ cup plain Greek yogurt 1
Tbsp. chopped parsley salt
and pepper

Cook the spelt in 2 ½ cup boiling water. Reduce the heat and cover after the water boils. Cook until the water evaporates and the grain is tender but not mushy.

Season the chicken with salt and pepper. Brown in a skillet coated with 2 Tbsp. olive oil. Cook about 7 minutes per side. Let the chicken cool.
The cooled chicken can be shredded or cut into bite size pieces.

Whisk together the 4 Tbsp. olive oil, lemon juice, and Greek yogurt. Season the dressing with salt and pepper.

Combine in a bowl: the chicken, the kale, carrots, tomatoes and ½ of the dressing.

Coat the grains with the rest of the dressing.

Place a mound of grains on each plate. On top of the grains, the seasoned chicken and vegetables.

Sprinkle parsley on the top and serve with the cheese.

## BARLEY, SPINACH AND MUSHROOMS

3 cup assorted wild mushrooms (oyster, cremini, shiitake), cleaned and sliced
1 lb. fresh baby spinach
1 medium sweet onion or 2 shallots, chopped
1 cup pearl barley (spelt would also be good)
3 cup water or chicken stock
¼ cup white wine or water or stock
1 Tbsp. olive oil
 thyme
salt and pepper
parmesan cheese

Bring liquid and barley to a boil. Cover and reduce heat to a simmer.
The barley is done when the liquid is absorbed, about 20 to 30 minutes on low heat.

While the barley is cooking, sauté the chopped onion.
Add the sliced mushroom and cook until tender.
Add the thyme, spinach and ¼ cup of liquid (wine or stock or water).
Cook UNCOVERED until the liquid is absorbed.

Add the mushrooms and spinach to the barley.
Season with salt, pepper and more thyme, if needed.

Serve with parmesan cheese.


## ALMOND QUINOA

1 cup quinoa
1 Tbsp. white wine vinegar
2 Tbsp. dry roasted almonds, coarsely chopped
1 Tbsp. lemon or orange juice
1 Tbsp. olive oil
salt and pepper

Add the 1cup of quinoa to 1½ cup water with a dash of salt and pepper.
Bring to a boil.
Reduce the heat and simmer until the liquid is absorbed, about 15b minutes.
Stir in the almonds, vinegar, citrus juice and 1Tbsp. of olive oil.
Season to taste.

**MY LAST RECIPE**

I started my memoir with a ketchup sauce for pasta. Since then, I have made countless varieties of pasta sauce, but I now have my most favorite. Just a tiny bit more work than ketchup, but really easy and I think terrific.

**PASTA SAUCE**

You can double, triple or make a vat. This is just right for four people, or two if it is Joe and Lynn.

½ sweet onion, cut into chunks

½ sweet red pepper, cut into chunks

2 carrots, peeled and cut into chunks*

½ fennel bulb, cleaned and cut into chunks

1 large can whole tomatoes with liquid

pepper and salt to taste.

*this is the most important of the vegetables. The carrots are what make this sauce! Add more if you like the sweet flavor.


Put all the ingredients into a pot and simmer until all the vegetables are soft.

Puree the whole thing in a food processor.

Simmer until ready to eat. Great on anything that calls for a tomato sauce.

***Tonight: pasta, sauce, shrimp, green salad and a nice glass of wine!***


That's it!!

RECIPE INDEX

**1960's**

| | |
|---|---|
| Elsie's Stuffed Cabbage | Page 11 |
| Washington Cherry Cake | Page 15 |
| Cannelloni: Pasta | Page 23 |
| Beef Roulades | Page 26 |
| Filet of Sole with Mushrooms | Page 29 |
| Mushroom Turnovers | Page 30 |
| Orange Cheesecake | Page 31 |
| Soupe Au Pistou | Page 36 |
| Apple Pie | Page 40 |
| Apricot Bread | Page 43 |
| Almond Bread | Page 43 |
| Tournadoes Rossini | Page 46 |

| | |
|---|---|
| Spinach Roll | Page 47 |
| Greek Style Meatballs | Page 48 |
| Eggplant Parmesan | Page 49 |
| Rugelach | Page 50 |

## 1970's

| | |
|---|---|
| Pâté | Page 53 |
| Beef Wellington | Page 54 |
| Salmon Coulibiac | Page 58 |
| Fish Pâté | Page 62 |
| Hunter's Chicken | Page 63 |
| Cannelloni: Crepes | Page 64 |
| Veal Orloff | Page 66 |
| Chicken Breasts with Mushrooms | Page 70 |
| Bagels | Page 71 |

Brown Rice, Rye, Millet and Beans		Page 72

Rice and Vegetables		Page 73

Frozen Cranberry- Pineapple Salad		Page 74

Lemon Squares		Page 75

Chocolate Raspberry Cake		Page 76

Dobosch Torte		Page 77

Brandy Alexander Pie		Page 78

Grasshopper Pie		Page 79

Pumpkin Flan		Page 80

## Late 1970's and 1980's

Two Tofu Recipes
- Carrots, Swiss Chard and Tofu		Page 87
- Tofu Noodle Soup		Page 88

Two Veggie Burgers
- Lentil Burgers		Page 89
- Nut and Grain		Page 89

| | |
|---|---|
| Lentil Pâté | Page 90 |
| Mac and Cheese | Page 91 |
| Mandarin Pancakes | Page 92 |

Moo Shi

| | |
|---|---|
| Lentil Casserole | Page 108 |

Pasta Sauces

| | |
|---|---|
| Roasted Tomato | Page 109 |
| Wild Mushroom | Page 109 |
| Sun Dried Tomatoes | Page 110 |
| Greens and Pine Nuts | Page 110 |
| Caponata | Page 111 |

Shrimp and Scallop Recipes

| | |
|---|---|
| Shrimp, Artichoke and Fennel | Page 112 |
| Scallops and Figs | Page 113 |
| Shrimp and Feta Cheese | Page 114 |
| Seafood Paella | Page 115 |
| Soft Polenta with Mushrooms | Page 116 |
| Spinach Torte | Page 117 |
| Zucchini "Charlotte" | Page 118 |

Chicken with Green Sauce          Page 120

Pastilla          Page 121

Muffins

    OMG: Way to Start the Day          Page 123

    Oat Pear          Page 124

    Ginger Pear          Page 124

    Apricot Peach          Page 125

    Cranberry Orange          Page 125

    Lemon Pecan          Page 126

Nuts For Apple Cake          Page 127

Lemon Yogurt Cake          Page 128

Two Thanksgiving Menus          Page 129

**1990's**

Savory Cakes

    Corn Fitters          Page 142

    Corn Cakes          Page 142

    Sweet Potato Cakes          Page 143

    Mushroom Cakes          Page 143

    Vegetable Cakes          Page 144

    Shrimp Cakes          Page 144

|  |  |
|---|---|
| Salmon/Shrimp Cakes | Page 145 |
| Salmon Corn Cakes | Page 145 |

Salad and Sauces that Accompany Savory Cakes

|  |  |
|---|---|
| Corn Salad | Page 146 |
| Ginger Cole Slaw | Page 146 |
| Carrot Salad | Page 146 |
| Root Vegetable Slaw | Page 147 |
| Beet, Carrot and Fennel | Page 147 |
| Zucchini and Fennel Slaw | Page 147 |
| Red Pepper Coulis | Page 148 |
| Cucumber and Mint Sauce | Page 148 |
| Salmon and Eggplant Dinner Party Menu | Page 149 |
| Winter Chicken Stew | Page 150 |
| Bouillabaisse Party Menu | Page 151 |
| Indian Inspired Menu | Page 153 |
| Low Fat Chocolate Cake | Page 154 |
| Chocolate Spiced Cookies | Page 155 |
| Three Thanksgiving Menus | Page 156 |

## 2000-2012

|  |  |
|---|---|
| Tea Smoked Chicken | Page 181 |

| | |
|---|---|
| Halibut | Page 182 |
| Swordfish | Page 183 |
| Monkfish, Fennel & Tomato | Page 184 |
| Fish Fillets with Green Sauce | Page 185 |
| Vegetarian Halloween Dinner | Page 186 |
| Mexican Inspired Dinner | Page 187 |
| Greek Dinner Menu | Page 189 |
| Vegetarian "Chef's" Dinner | Page 190 |
| Pork Roast Dinner Party | Page 196 |
| Thanksgiving Menu | Page 197 |
| New Year's Eve | Page 198 |

**2012**

Salads for Pot Luck Suppers			Page 203

Cold Buffet Dinner Party			Page 205

Thanksgiving Menu				Page 206

**2013-2014**

FISH

| | |
|---|---|
| Cod with Lemon, Peppers anc Olives | Page 212 |
| Fish with Corriander, Cumin and Yogurt | Page 213 |
| Steamed Salmon | Page 214 |
| Miso Salmon | Page 215 |
| Salmon, Eggplant Stacks | Page 215 |
| Herring | Page 216 |
| Roasted Trout with Lentils and Verjus | Page 217 |
| Greek Style Fish | Page 218 |
| Halibut | Page 219 |
| Halibut with Zucchini and Carrots | Page 220 |
| Trout with Harcots Verts and Almonds | Page 221 |
| Trout with Preserved Lemon Vinaigrette | Page 222 |
| Tuna Kabobs | Page 223 |

## VEGETABLES

| | |
|---|---|
| Butternut Squash/Sweet Potatoes Cakes | Page 224 |
| Roasted Carrots and Yogurt | Page 224 |
| Roasted Sweet Potato Slices | Page 225 |
| Sweet Potato and Kale Pizza | Page 225 |
| Sweet Potato with Orange and Nuts | Page 226 |
| Sweet Potato Pancakes | Page 226 |
| Sweet Potato Spread | Page 227 |
| Pumpkin, Bean and Mushroom Ragu | Page 227 |
| Beet Burger | Page 228 |
| Carrots and Oranges | Page 229 |
| Butternut Squash and Apples | Page 230 |
| Cauliflower and Carrot Puree | Page 231 |
| Cooking Greens | Page 232 |
| Escarole, Kale and Bok Choy | Page 233 |
| Roasting Vegetables | Page 234 |
| Sauteed Brussels Sprouts /Almonds and Currants | Page 235 |
| Stuffed Kale | Page 235 |
| Salads | Page 236 |
| Kale, Brussels Sprouts, Chinese Cabbage | Page 238 |
| Roasted Brussels Sprouts and Apples | Page 238 |

## GRAINS

| | |
|---|---|
| Spelt and Chicken Salad | Page 239 |
| Barley Spinach and Mushrooms | Page 240 |
| Almond Quinoa | Page 240 |

# MY LAST RECIPE

| | |
|---|---|
| PASTA SAUCE, quick and delicious! | Page 241 |

Made in the USA
Middletown, DE
31 July 2015